TERRI HOOLEY: SEVENTY-FIVE REVOLUTIONS

Stuart Baillie

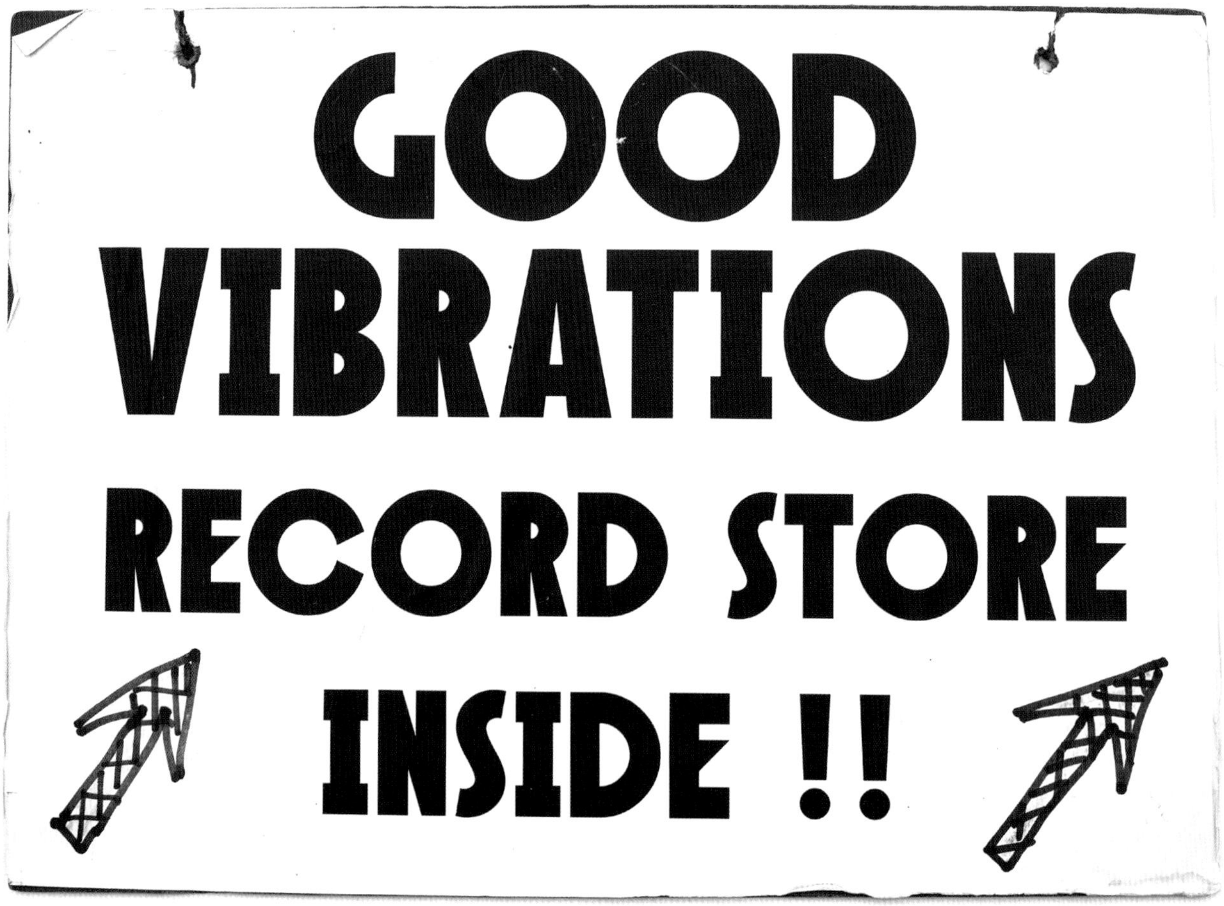
GOOD
VIBRATIONS
RECORD STORE
INSIDE !!

TERRI HOOLEY:

BY STUART BAILIE

SEVENTY-FIVE

WITH A FOREWORD BY TERRI HOOLEY

REVOLUTIONS

Designed by Betsy Bailie

dig with it.

I too am not a bit tamed,
I too am untranslatable,
I sound my barbaric yawp
over the roofs of the world.

Walt Whitman

"People said if you walked
down the Ormeau Road on
the right-hand side at night,
you were a Catholic. If you
walked on the left-hand
side, you were a Protestant.
But Terri Hooley and his
band of merry men always
danced down the middle."

Terri Hooley

Carrie Davenport

ISBN 978-1-3999-6848-5
Printed by Akcent Media

Contents:

Terri by Anto Brennan

Cliff Mason

Foreword by Terri Hooley

When Stuart first mentioned about doing a photographic book I thought he was joking. Nobody knows more about my life than Stuart. He knows more about my life than I can remember. His book *Trouble Songs* was a great success and is now regarded as the definitive book about songs written about the conflict.

When *Trouble Songs* was first published, he did an interview with the *Irish News* and they asked him, 'Who is your best friend and where did you meet?' Stuart said it was me and that I had turned down his first punk band but that we had made our peace in 1980 and every Friday we have breakfast in Skinner's in Holywood and talk about the revolution. I was surprised to read this as I thought for all those years we had had an ongoing exchange of opposite views. Maybe we have both mellowed over the years, but our politics have not. I am in awe of Stuart as he is brilliant at everything he does. His *Dig With It* magazine is my favourite publication in Ireland and like this book is designed by his very talented daughter Betsy.

My life has been full of big highs and even bigger lows but has never been boring. I have been lucky to have had so many wonderful friends on my life's journey. Some people say that I never do what people expect me to do and that I go off on tangents. But I believe my tangents have led to some of the things I am most proud of. Colin McClelland, the editor of a Sunday newspaper, said in a discussion about the 60s, 'Back then, Terri Hooley jumped on every bandwagon going, but he did it a year before any of us heard about it'.

The 60s was a great era for me as a young teenager when, if you had the money, you could go to nearly 80 places in and around Belfast to hear music. From little church halls to huge ballrooms with revolving stages. My history does not start with the Battle of the Boyne in 1690, but in 1965, going out on a Friday night with some friends to the Spanish Rooms on the Falls Road. Buying a gallon of scrumpy for £1 and drinking it up an alley. We would take the plastic container back and get 1/6 and then buy a £1 deal of hashish between us before going to the Maritime to hear the wonderful Them. If you met a girl and got a wee lumber, that was the cherry on top.

Music has always been my passion, starting off being a DJ, then running folk and blues clubs, being a pirate radio broadcaster, running psychedelic clubs like Underground Art and the Middle Earth, putting out alternative magazines like *ID* and *Ego*, and of course the Good Vibrations shop and record label. A music journalist said to me some years ago, 'Terri, you were the man who made possible John Peel's all-time favourite record - you never have to do anything else'.

I never thought anyone would ever remember the things we did years ago and would never have believed that a film and a musical would be made about my life. When the musical was on at the Lyric Theatre to sold-out audiences and standing ovations, the director Des Kennedy said, 'They come in here with walking sticks and Zimmer frames and the next thing they are up dancing in the aisles. We are the new Lourdes!'

Now, I am living a quiet life in Bangor with Claire and Amber, the one-eyed wonder rescue dog, and spend three days a week on dialysis and choose my battles very carefully. It was when I was the 17-year-old Chairman of the Northern Ireland Youth Campaign for Peace and Nuclear Disarmament and the Belfast Council for Peace in Vietnam that I learned not to trust governments. Especially the Americans, who continually lied to their own people about their involvement in Vietnam. I can't understand why in the past America and Russia have banned me. After all, I am not dangerous - just a washed-out old peaceful anarchist hippy, even though I say I am a fake and a fraud.

On the last night of the musical at the Lyric, I said:

THE FIGHT IS NOT OVER & WILL NEVER BE OVER UNTIL WE BEAT THE BIGOTS, THE RACISTS AND THE HOMOPHOBIC BASTARDS.

Terri's Dedications

Claire Archibald, my guardian angel, who has spoilt me rotten and been keeping me alive for years. Eithne McIlroy and Michael Hooley, Ugne Dinsmonaite, Ruth and Anna Carr, Laura Hale my special friend, my nieces Jacqui and Justine Hooley, Ben Clegg. Stevie 'Boy' Nicholl, Michael Callaghan and Keike Twisselmann, Gary Lightbody, Jimmy Symington and Shantala Porter, Alister Beverley, Bryan Collis, Bob Kildea, Jonny Quinn, Nathan Connolly and Sarah Green. Frankie Quinn, Sean McKernan, Melanie Harrison, Joanne and Neil Cameron, Jim Reilly, Kerry Gooding, Arthur Magee, Sean Kelly, Biggy Bigmore, Barry Phillips, Rob Aiken, Brenda and Wee Doc. Bronagh Gallagher, Louise Gallagher, Martin, Fiontan and Ella McAleavey, Brixton Nick, Leslie Anderson, Darren Chittick, John and Dorothy Waid, John Carson, Carolyn Mathers and Cathy McCullough, Charlotte Dryden and all the great people at Oh Yeah. Glenn Patterson and Colin Carberry, Chris Martin. Jimmy Fay, Des Kennedy, Claire Murray, Catherine and Gloria (from Skinner's), Joanne and Colin (from Truffles), Natasa Kokic, Steven and Jean Shaw, Gerry and Vivien Gleason, Frankie Connolly, Nuala Kirk, Roy and Carole Hill, Buck and Sharon Murdock, Aidan Murtagh, Robin and Pauline Elliott, Dave Hyndman, Rachel Tooher, Pedro and Michael Donald. Gerry White, Richard Dormer, Aaron McCusker, Glen Wallace, Glenn Leyburn and Lisa Barros D'Sa, David Holmes and Lisa Di Lucia, Martin Corrigan, Lee McKillen, Owen McFadden, Davy and Dawn Sims, Davy Matchett, Suzanne Doyle, Ken Lotery, Libby Irvine, Cait O'Riordan, Ian McTear, Sharon Hall and Darragh MacIntyre, Kim Turtle, Darrin and Julie Robson, Karen Turner, Caroline McDonnell and the girls from the north country, Cait Higgins, Aidy and Catherine McAllister, Rosie Blair, Lee Hedley, Anthony Toner, Jess Dunleavy, Bernie McAllister, Gerry McNally, Chris Flack, Mireia and Pablo Buckler, Annette Burgers, Erwin Blom and Roeland Stekelenburg, Ian Morrison, Mario Goossens and Karel Miles. Conor Garrett, Tina Catling and Mark Davies, Lady Portia. All my lovely girls in Boots, Beersbridge Road, Belfast. Dr. Fogarty, Dr. Woodman and all the nurses in the Renal Unit, Ulster Hospital, Dr. McCauley and the staff of University St. Surgery, the cast of *Good Vibrations*, the musical. Everyone on the Good Vibrations record label.

Terri Hooley Timeline

1948 Terence Wilfred Hooley is born on 23 December at 11 Cameron Street, Belfast. He spends his early years at 22 Glenluce Drive in the Garnerville estate before moving to 12 Hillfoot Street in east Belfast. **1954** Terri is accidentally shot by an arrow and loses his left eye. **1977** Opens Good Vibrations record shop at 102 Great Victoria Street, Belfast. **1978** Starts Good Vibrations Records. The first release is 'Big Time' by RUDI; the fourth is 'Teenage Kicks' by The Undertones. **1983** Good Vibrations goes bankrupt, but the shop will return in many guises and at 11 locations. **2012** The film *Good Vibrations* is released, with Richard Dormer in the role of Terri Hooley and Jodie Whittaker as his wife Ruth. **2012** A plaque is unveiled on Hill Street, Belfast to mark the site of the old Harp Bar, the punk bands that played there and the legacy of Terri Hooley. **2018** *Good Vibrations*, the stage musical, is launched at the Lyric Theatre, Belfast. **2023** A Lyric Theatre production of *Good Vibrations* is restaged at the Grand Opera House, Belfast, before moving to the Irish Center, New York.

Introduction
by Stuart Bailie

Terri Hooley is a poet, a fool, an upsetter and a hallion. He deals in truth, fables and blarney. He's been a friend for 40 years and he still surprises. He can play it light and evasive, which are handy skills in Belfast when people want to box you in. There are also times when he reveals a bedrock of heart and belief.

You may know him from *Good Vibrations* – the film and the stage musical. He was thrilled by punk rock in Belfast and released some brilliant records on the label that he named after his shop – itself named after a Beach Boys song. You can read about Terri in tabloid papers and academic studies. Social media is busy with admiring words and a few snarky takedowns. Hooley's belief in the power of the seven-inch single has created life changes for many thousands of us. Belfast has a plaque, a mural and a tree that celebrates his work. There's a portrait by Colin Davidson that pushes the paint into a thoughtful expression. Terri jokes that it's only a matter of time before someone stages *Good Vibrations on Ice* – the ultimate, feel-good spectacle.

But first, here is *75 Revolutions*, my own tilt at the life story. The original idea was to create a photo book – trying to capture that face and all the life experiences that made it. But then the words came with the images and I looked to my archive of interviews and adventures. The pair of us have been hilariously lost in Liverpool, Brussels, Dublin and London. For a bunch of years, we played tunes together at Voodoo every Thursday night in Belfast. We've had moments of tremendous, 3am insight, which neither of us can remember well. And when the buffoonery stops, there has been sorrow and solidarity.

This is a version of the man as he approaches a great birthday. One of my interests is to locate Terri in the now. After 75 rotations around the sun, how does it *feel*?

Johnny Cash showed us how you can engage and resonate in every period of your life. It can all mean something. The best way to explore this is to search out the riffs, the reasons and the vibrations. Let's try it.

Stuart Bailie
September 2023

Breakfast at Skinner's

I meet Terri every week at Skinner's café in Holywood, County Down. We put in the same order and the tea is always served up with the food. We might have cheerful stories to share. Often, we moan, mither and bitch. Sometimes we talk about revolution.

For many years, Skinner's was a Friday morning routine. It was a starter for the weekend, a moment of lightness. Yet in March 2023, Terri's health started to worsen. His kidneys were in a bad way and the doctors said that they couldn't suspend the dialysis treatment any longer.

They made their decision on the morning of March 29. But Terri told the consultants that it was the tenth anniversary of *Good Vibrations* – the film about his life. He was due to attend a special screening at The Strand cinema in east Belfast that evening. His friends all had tickets. He couldn't disappoint. Luckily, some of the hospital team were also fans of the film. They had enjoyed this alternative story of teenage thrills and punk noise during the conflict. So they patched him up, gave him an injection and Hooley was duly despatched to the pictures.

There was some confusion in the foyer as Terri's friends had heard different versions of the day's events. A couple of mates had prepared back-up speeches while others were convinced that the main man was a no-show. In the old days, Hooley might have disappeared for three days at a time and this kind of turbulence was a given. As a young man, his GP had warned him that he might never live to see 30. But the party years are seemingly over. Terri has survived a few heart-attacks, a mini-stroke and pneumonia. His constitution has served him well but now there are limits.

Earlier in the spring, he had even convinced the doctors that he might fly to New York in June to watch the opening night of the *Good Vibrations* stage musical at the Irish Center. The travel insurance premium was going to be high, but the promoters were aiming to make it work. Unfortunately, the medical results in March were not so positive. Terri was allowed out to see the film at The Strand, on condition that he returned to the hospital directly afterwards. So he took a car ride to the Holywood Road, stopping in front of the cinema. No red carpet, but the marquee sign announced the show and Terri stood under the letters in his trademark Crombie overcoat.

13

When they took him back to the hospital, he contracted Covid. Then the haemodialysis line in his chest got infected and continued to bleed. He had lost some weight and there was due concern. Yet on May 10, he made it down to the Grand Opera House in Belfast for the press night of the *Good Vibrations* musical. And he saw the show again at the end of the run – when the acting was more assured and the audience was singing and whooping.

When the show moved to New York in the summer, the cast sent Terri video messages and clips of the audience reaction. Morale was high, press cuttings were upbeat and Manhattan liked it. As with the film, Terri's story translated well on the stage. It was about a little guy in a twisted society. He pushes back and he provides example. Yet this great effort exacts a price. It exposes his weaknesses and provokes a fall.

Good Vibrations has become mythic and relatable. Some life details have been tweaked and altered for this purpose. It is not simply a narrative about a 30-year period in Northern Ireland when around 3,600 were killed in a vicious mess. In Moscow, they loved the part in the film when Terri calls the Dave Hyndman character a 'Stalinist'. In Austin, Texas, they applauded at the mention of their local band, The 13th Floor Elevators.

The rest of us will never see our lives amplified in this way. Terri watches the scenes when paramilitary thugs rough him up for not paying protection money. He took a terrible beating in real life and he flinches as he watches it. Likewise, he did actually escape from a murder gang at a time when random killings were frequent and the corpses of friends were being dumped in alleyways.

'I cried the first time I saw it,' he remembers. 'I still cry every time I see it. And then I realise what a dick I was and that I drank so much. But I think the film is about freedom. It could be any trouble spot in the world, a universal story. It could be Latin America or Palestine or Israel – anywhere that people have had enough and want to do something different.'

After a performance of the stage version at the Lyric Theatre, Terri was approached by some former members of the paramilitary gang that had beaten him up. They came with their wives and brought him cards, inscribed with contrite messages. They said they were sorry for what they had done.

In the film version of *Good Vibrations*, many details were telescoped and the script suggested that he had left his wife Ruth, shortly after the birth of their daughter Anna. Rewrites of the theatrical version have made it clear that there was more than 18 months between the birth and the break-up. Terri has not said much about artistic embellishment, although he does quote from other parts of the script. 'Raise your expectations,' is a favourite. So too is the line, 'we're music people' – chiefly used when media sorts try to schedule an early morning meeting.

Hooley in the 70s was raucous figure. He had a freewheeling, beatnik manner and he did not defer to power-brokers and gate-keepers. My own generation was younger by a dozen years. We had grown up in conflict and had little self-worth. But Terri had heard the chimes of freedom and he would not forget. I remember him at venues like The Harp Bar and The Pound, a 30-year-old guy, shouting into the microphone, urging us to see greatness in ourselves. On many occasions, he was drunk and the words landed badly. But on a good night, it was like a punk rock edition of *Henry V*, rousing the kids, prepping them with power chords and insolence, ready to charge the breach.

Stuart Bailie

I frequented his shop on Great Victoria Street and was inspired by Terri's releases on the Good Vibrations label, especially those early ones by RUDI, The Undertones and Protex. I formed a band and like many of the second generation of new wavers, we expected that Terri would provide. We didn't have the self-awareness to know that we were too late and too derivative. On one occasion, Ian, our drummer visited the shop on Great Victoria Street to convince the man of the band's worth. He saw Terri, stretched out on the shop counter. Ian gave the guy his spiel about the potential greatness of Acme Music. No response. In time, he realised that he had been talking to Terri's glass eye, but its owner was sleeping off a bad hangover. The Hooleygan woke up and opened his good eye. He scratched his beard, lit a Benson & Hedges and headed back to the pub. Oh well.

'That was the old Terri Hooley,' is his refrain now. True, his lifestyle is more temperate, but for someone approaching 75, he is a character with form. He tends not to edit his thoughts. The internal policeman in his brain works randomly - the frontal lobe is mostly off-duty. Which can feel a bit disconcerting, even now. You can never rely on a polite response.

Terri was fortunate when he found his tribe as a hippy-anarchist. A decade later, he delighted in the chaos and fever of punk. He saw that there were common themes. Bigotry is wrong. Capitalism is a problem, not a fix. He doesn't follow leaders and the rare appearance of cash makes him uncomfortable.

His stubborn side took him through bomb blasts, bankruptcy, violent attacks and arson. He kept shop in a variety of places - he reckons as many as 11 locations in all. In his senior years, he's been teaching us another lesson - the job of divestment. He has few possessions and much of his music memorabilia was consumed in the North Street Arcade fire of 2004. He's content to be away from the centre of the local music community, especially the begrudgers in the dimly lit bars. He moved to Bangor, County Down with his partner Claire two years ago.

'I never thought that would happen,' he admits. 'Gary Lightbody says I live and breathe Belfast. I've always loved it. I haven't always loved what's happened in Belfast. But I've always thought Belfast was a great place. I'm not sure if my love affair is what it used to be. I think it might be time to move on, and grow old gracefully, instead of disgracefully. I think I retired years ago and just didn't tell anybody.'

Since the dialysis sessions started, we organise our breakfast visits to Skinner's around his treatment days. Terri is careful about his intake of food and fluids, but the humour is back. Claire is resigned to the idea that Terri only cares for '50s food'. He dislikes the avocado, the side salad and even brown bread. He enjoys a bit of disrespect with his table service and still talks about the pure contempt he got in a north Belfast café when he asked for a fry without baked beans. He loved the honesty of the transaction.

He wraps up the last of his sausage in a napkin. He will bring it home for Amber, the rescue dog. Like Terri, she has lost her left eye. His thoughts ramble and he talks about the erotic vision of his aunt's corsage. There's another story about Toots Hibbert and his underwear. He remembers the night he took liquid acid as a teenager and sat up for hours with his mother, Mavis, telling her all his secrets. 'It was the most incredible conversation I ever had with my mum. She was very supportive.' And while his father was a stern, principled socialist and trade unionist, there was a moment when he returned from a record sale at Caroline Music with a couple of purchases. George Hooley would vacuum the house as he played 'Sun City' by Artists United Against Apartheid. Another soundtrack to his cleaning chores was a 12-inch pressing of 'Atmosphere'.

'Atmosphere' by Joy Division?

'No, 'Atmosphere' by Russ Abbot.'

He has a scar below his nose, testimony to a childhood altercation with a boy called Eddie, who came at him with a bottle. There's some historic damage to his leg after an angry lover stabbed him with a knife, requiring stitches.

Most times, he keeps his artificial eye in the socket it was designed for. But many of us have spent post-party mornings rummaging around sofa cushions, ash trays and shag pile rugs for the missing item. Terri and his prosthetic are a tremendous double act. I remember a rough morning in Brussels when the eye was absent and then I noticed it, stuck to Hooley's forearm, staring me out.

His voice has been loosened by cigarettes, porter and brandy. He speaks with inflections from the rough streets of Belfast. But his talk is also sprung like music and he adds little camp flourishes, a throwback to 60s counterculture, to Dylan, Jagger and the school of Warhol, a measure of otherness and sly rebellion.

Breakfast at Skinner's is sweet and humdrum. We repeat old stories and punchlines, like characters in a Harold Pinter play. We go over the playlists for Terri's online radio show on Belfast 247. There might be mention of family issues and the dreary condition of local party politics. And if the weather is decent, we visit the charity shops, always astonished that CDs are selling for 50p when the original retail price was £15. We buy up Gram Parsons, Prince Buster and Edith Piaf for the drive home.

Recently, we were in the Assisi Animal Sanctuary shop when a tune started to play. It was 'Please Stay' by The Cryin' Shames. A song about beautiful desperation. The boy who's singing it has no pride left. He just doesn't want the girl to leave him again. This was the last record that Joe Meek produced, and it sounds like it's come from a weird dimension. It was a hit in 1966 and Terri is lost in recollection. Then we nod. The popular song enthrals us yet.

He is still wistful as we walk down High Street and take a right on Church Road. He's looking at the boarded-up shops and estate agent signs. I believe I know what is on his mind. Terri Hooley is still dreaming about record shops.

'I still dream about setting up record shops. I have no sense at all.'

At 75

So, as Terri Hooley reaches 75, is it a time for reflection?

I just can't believe I'm still alive. I go to bed every night and say my mantra. It comes from the *Magic Roundabout* film *Dougal and the Blue Cat*: 'Be content with what you've got, 'cos what you've got is quite a lot.'

I would say I've never been as happy as I am now. Truly. I always had this empty feeling, a real sadness inside. For years and years and years. I think it stems back to my youth. People dying on me – it wasn't very nice of them to leave me on my own. And now it's gone. I'm very lucky that I'm so happy. And it's not a strange feeling. It only took me 70 years to be happy. I'm quite enjoying old age.

When I say I used to be the loneliest kid in the bedroom, it wasn't that I didn't have friends, or anything. But it just didn't feel that we had the same interests. But records were like my friends. My imaginary friends. I met someone I used to know and he was coming from the Masonic meeting one night and he said, "We used to laugh at you Terri, and all your weird music like Leonard Cohen and Joni Mitchell". He says, "Now we're buying those CDs".

Janis Ian sang 'I learnt the truth at 17'. Do you learn any truth when you're 75?

Aye – don't do the stupid things that you did the last time. I'm sorry that I ever set up a record label (laughs). I could have done something with my life.

So much has happened in the past ten years. Particularly, the *Good Vibrations* film and then the stage musical. How do you digest that?

When I saw the film, I thought it was Richard Dormer's story. And I cry every time. It's just very strange. I really have to pinch myself. I always felt I was destined to do something but I didn't think it would be what I did. I thought I'd be writing my prison diaries by now. This is the thing I feel disappointed with. I've had wonderful friends. Unfortunately, a lot of them died young, and when I saw the film, I thought "Oh God, I wish that such-and-such was alive. They would have loved this film. They would have been so proud."

Good Vibrations was such a huge success at the Lyric. It was sold out every night, a standing ovation every night. It was one of the most successful things they're had in years. So they were dying to get it back. Even the front-of-house staff were going, "This is brilliant, we love it". In fact, some people like the play better

than the film. One camp loves the film, and then another camp loves the play. I loved the play.

But there are a lot of things I have to thank for in my life. The people who worked in Good Vibrations, the people who helped to set it up. The people who were always there during the Troubles, guarding my back. I had some really good friends, and I miss them. Even the ones that I rarely see these days.

I'm not very good at keeping in touch with people. I just got a message from an old friend in New Zealand. He said, "I've just watched *Good Vibrations* and I'm thinking about you".

I mean, I met a lot of lunatics. I used to get all these mad people coming over from England. Some of them, you didn't know if they were police spies or not.

Did you like the script for *Good Vibrations*?

All the intelligent stuff, I didn't say.

It created an international awareness of your life. How was that?

I really mean this – I honestly never thought anybody would ever remember those things. I still meet people who go, "I've still got all your magazines". I say, "Well, I haven't got them all". Or people show me ticket stubs for the Ulster Hall.

Some of the details of your life have changed across the narrative of the film and the stage musical. Does that process bother you?

Well, when I hear stories now of my past, I go, hold on, that's the old Terri, this is the new, reborn Terri. We don't talk about the old Terri.

But there are many variations on the story of the old Terri...

Jesus Christ, for ten years I've suffered from, "Did you not go to your daughter's birth?" I was not allowed at the birth. No fathers were. There were major works going on in the maternity. And that afternoon (5 September 1979) I wasn't out partying with Siouxsie and the Banshees. I actually saved their concert. Their PA was stuck in Liverpool because all the roadies got pissed the night before and missed the boat. There was no PA in Northern Ireland but I got a firm in Dublin who said they would come up for me. And I'd taken The Cure down to do an interview in Downtown (Radio).

I was phoning every hour (the City Hospital) to see how Ruth was and then at 12 at the Ulster Hall they told me not to call again. In the morning, I got a phone from the hospital – mother and baby are doing well. Fifteen minutes later I was at the hospital and I wasn't allowed in. They said, "Come back tomorrow at visiting time". So, it wasn't that I didn't take any interest in the birth of my daughter (Anna).

And my daughter played the nurse (in the film) who brought her into the world, which I thought was a bit strange. She said to me, "Daddy, did you not hold me when I was in hospital?" I says, "Darling, this is not a documentary. This is a film."

In the recent TV documentary series Once Upon a Time in Northern Ireland you repeat the line that you didn't kill anyone during the conflict. That was a powerful moment.

That's the truth. I always wanted to be able to say to my children – or my grandchildren – when they said, "Daddy, what did you do during the Troubles?" I wanted to say, "Well, I partied a lot, and I drank a lot and I did drugs, and I had a good time. And I never killed anybody." Because a lot of people I knew did go out and they did bomb people, and they did shoot people.

I had thought about killing myself at one point. I had a double-barrelled shotgun behind the pipes in our bathroom, which was given to me by a friend. She stole it out of her uncle's garage. It was beautiful German engineering, a Krupp shotgun. I actually thought, "Fuck this, I'm gonna kill myself". But then the girls came and said to me, "Come on, we're going to a party out in Lisburn".

Claire Archibald

I went to collect my friend Tommy. They said, "Go up to the bedroom". So I knocked the door. Tommy had a stick and a noose, lying on the bed. I said, "What the fuck are you doing?" He said, "I've had enough, I can't take any more". I says, "Come on, we're going to a party, fuck that".

We went to this party and found this big carry-out and a lump of hashish behind the sofa and we partied on. At eight in the morning we were getting the bus to go to work. I says, "We're not going to work, I don't care if it's payday. I'm phoning in, telling them I'm not well."

So, I had Room 5a, 53 High St (an office space in town that Terri used in the late 60s). We found a Batman-themed record. We went and got some cider and then we found some silver paper and we wrapped the bottle. We thought we were drinking champagne. I just said, "I can't do that nine-to-five thing. I don't want to be like everybody else. I don't want to be a worker ant. I just want to have fun." And then we partied all weekend. That was the morning when I just thought, "Fuck this, I'm not working for the Man".

When *Good Vibrations* was staged at the Lyric Theatre, you were approached by some ex-paramilitaries who had once attacked you. What happened?

I think I've got the card somewhere. I think it's all about forgiveness. There were two different people. Both had turned Christian and they apologised for the attacks. They gave me this card about forgiveness. But I'm glad they did it.

There was a time I went into prison and talked to the loyalists. I said to them, "By the way, I'm a Sandy Row Methodist, I'm not a Fenian". And all they wanted to know about was Johnny Adair's punk band. I said to them, "This has been a very interesting afternoon, I'm glad I came – I'm gonna go down to the John Hewitt and drink a pint of Guinness and a brandy. And I wish yous all the best. But I hope I never see your fucking ugly faces again." And they all cheered. So I went to the John Hewitt and I saw an old friend. He says, "Terri, I haven't seen you for ages". I says, "I'm just out of prison".

But it was just the hatred. If you look at *Once Upon a Time in Northern Ireland*, it's the hatred. You hear it on the radio. People say, "Oh, I couldn't meet a Catholic". What the fuck? What sort of world are they living in?

Your old associate David Hyndman says you're the only person from that era who hasn't changed.

Aye, 'cos I'm still as stupid as ever. People don't realise that I am as thick as a brick. I didn't even get sitting the 11-plus. I was told at school I wouldn't even get a job sweeping the streets, I was that thick. So that's why I liked the idea of trying to put Northern Ireland back on the music map, and I liked the idea of giving kids a chance. To get out there and play in bands, and a chance to maybe travel to England and stuff. It was up to them to do the rest, but I liked the idea of getting people the opportunity of doing things that I hadn't done, and maybe seeing the world.

Any regrets that you didn't broker any music deals for yourself, like percentages or finder's fees?

No, I've never regretted that. I've always hated the music industry with a passion. When I think of all the blues guys and the way they were treated... I mean, people had never heard of John Lee Hooker and Muddy Waters until the British Invasion, but they were our heroes.

So you're comfortable enough?

I'm happy enough. I grew up in poverty. I've never been as rich, actually. I've just bought five pairs of socks. But the thing is, people who have inherited money and all, it's just the worst thing ever happened to them. So money never really interested me. What you never had, you never miss.

What do you dream of when you dream about record shops?

I just couldn't open a record shop again, but I still dream about them. I don't understand why I can't dream about being in bed with beautiful women. I'm wired up wrong. I'm sorting out the racks and discovering warehouses of records that have been lying there empty – that nobody's touched for years – and packing them up and sending them to Belfast and then putting them out. I wouldn't go home until all the records were priced and put out. I'd be changing the display in the window and all. I dream about it all the time.

Opposite:
Image by
Stuart Bailie

Bronagh Gallagher

I was at St Mary's, a fantastic school (in Derry), and we were going to Belfast to see Queen's University for the Open Day. By this stage, I was into Muddy Waters and Howlin' Wolf and Blind Willie and it was just like, "Where do I get these records?" Because you could order them here in Derry but I wanted to get them 'cos I had a few quid - my ma gave me a fiver or something. So I made a beeline in my blue uniform, with my coat over it, up to Terri Hooley.

He said, "Where are you from, where's that uniform from?" I said, "I'm from Derry" and I said, "Have you any Muddy Waters?" And he said, "What do you call you?" And I said, "Bronagh" and we started chatting. He wasn't very friendly - he was grumpy - but we blathered away anyway and I got the *Live at Mr. Kelly's* by Muddy Waters, and I nearly wore a hole in it. We connected that day

and he remembered me when my mum and Louise (Bronagh's sister) and I went up again another time. Louise went to Belfast for a meeting for the BBC, which she then got into and spent 23 years in it, and so we befriended Terri Hooley. He had no choice. We just got him under the arm in a headlock. So that was it.

He had great soul stuff and great blues, obviously, great reggae and then the punk and the great girl bands. He had The Shangri-Las and he had The Ronettes blaring and when you went in he was there, smoking away. And it was like, "I have that, and my mammy has that - have you got this?" So you met your tribe - this is it, I'm not moving. The thought of getting back on the bus to Derry was heartbreaking. But I knew I could get the records up there too - Freda Payne, 'Band of Gold' - got that in Derry. And I think there was a bit of Sheena Easton in there too because I was only a wee'an.

Terri, Charlotte Dryden and Bronagh Gallagher, 2010. Image by Carrie Davenport.

But just getting those records that Terri had – he knew the guys to send you to because he knew the blues, the Chess and the Stax. My mammy had a certain amount of records that I wasn't really allowed to wreck or take away because they were special records – all Atlantic that she would have bought at the time. So, once you had your own money and you could go up, you were getting all the gear on you and going up to Belfast, shopping for the day. Three hours it took then, before the Maiden City Flyer. Up on the bus and into Good Vibrations, that was it, and you'd go and get a sandwich then, get the shopping in and then back up the road. Oh aye, with a record – boom – and then that was it.

You had The Outcasts. And you obviously had Stiff Little Fingers, but they were an international band, they were real stars. But he was the scene in Belfast also. I mean, we wouldn't have been allowed to go up until we were about 17. Then I would have went up and stayed with my sister, so then you would have went to the gigs and up to Lavery's (Bar) and all the punks would have hung out. But the shop was where the punks hung out. Just visually, what you were going in to see. Derry had its own scene too, but if you wanted the records and you wanted to branch out, you were going to Belfast to hang out with the dudes.

No More Darkness

Terri fell in love with his first record in 1952. It was Hank Williams and 'I Saw the Light'. A song about being saved from a life filled with sin. About travelling on the way that is narrow, through the gate that is straight.

Hank Williams sang it with the fervour of the born-again while the Drifting Cowboys played beside him like it was an old-time tent revival. Hank was a hard drinker, a pill-eater and a womaniser, but all this salvation was licence for the Hillbilly Shakespeare. The song had been inspired by a late-night journey home from a gig in Alabama. Hank's mother Lily was driving the band and she noticed the illuminations of the airfield by their hometown of Montgomery. She woke her drunken son. 'I just saw the light,' she said. Hank changed a casual remark into a great work of testimony and put it out into the world in 1948, the year when Terri was born.

He first heard the tune in a guest house in Botanic Avenue, south Belfast. Some of the people who stopped there were theatrical types, booked in for a run at the Grand Opera House. Later, they said that Gene Vincent, bringer of 'Be-Bop-a-Lula', was a guest. The two women who ran the establishment were fixing up breakfasts on a Sunday morning and unable to attend their Methodist church. So Terri's grandfather, George Wilson, used to walk around the corner from 11 Cameron Street on a Friday and collect their weekly offerings.

Terri was tagging along with George and he witnessed the ceremony of a record being played. The Hank Williams record was heavy and fragile. Once every minute, the shellac disc made 78 rotations on the turntable. The label had the bright yellow livery and the black roaring lion of MGM Records, a subsidiary of the film studio. It sounded fantastic.

'I just fell in love with it. I begged and begged them to play it over and over again. They had to drag me away. And that was my first musical memory, and my first hero, and my favourite country-gospel song. That just changed my life. And from that point I wanted to hear every bit of music in the world.'

'I Saw the Light' had an extra resonance in the summer of 1954. Terri's neighbour in the Garnerville estate was aiming a bow and arrow at a biscuit tin, trying to knock it off the wall. But the arrow rebounded and struck Terri, damaging his left eye. He was rushed to the Royal Victoria Hospital but the vision in his eye could not be saved.

Mavis Hooley

Terri and John Hooley

'I don't think I realised at the time it was quite so bad. My mum was in the Red Cross and she bandaged me up. But then they came and changed the dressing around my eyes. They were walking me out to the ambulance and it was a lovely, sunny day and the sun was shining through the bandages. I was thinking, "These ambulance men, they are stupid" – all they had to do was bandage up one eye and I could walk out. And then I was thinking about Hank Williams and 'I Saw the Light'.

'I stayed in the hospital and I just wanted to go home. And I remember my mum collecting me, and I was so glad to get out. We went across the road to the wee park and my mum pushed me on the swing. And I remember the freedom of being out of hospital. I just thought, "This is great".'

His mother, Mavis, was a Sandy Row Methodist. 'My mum was so religious that when she went into town shopping, she used to go to Saint Mary's chapel in Smithfield and pray. Because all the Protestant churches were closed. Before my mother died, I said to her, "If anyone deserves to get to Heaven, it's you. And I'm sure you'll be very welcome." She was a good woman.'

Mavis' father was renting out rooms and had sent her into town to place a new classified ad in the *Belfast Telegraph*. On her way past Shaftesbury Square, Mavis met George Hooley, a serviceman from Staffordshire who was on duty in Belfast. He had previously served

in the Merchant Navy, experiencing the dread of the Atlantic convoys, when 3,500 merchant ships and 175 warships were sunk, many of them destroyed by German U-boats. He had been stationed in India and Borneo and spent the later part of his service in the Royal Irish Fusiliers. Like many of his generation, he was reticent about his war years and any of the ill effects.

'He didn't really talk about the war. My mum and him went on holiday to Italy and they went to Monte Cassino, to visit the graveyard for the fallen. After about six rows, my dad saw his brother's grave and turned white. That's how I found out that I had an uncle that was killed in the war.

'I always found out stories – like, I didn't know my father was in the Atlantic convoys. And he was telling this friend of mine that when he went to Houston, Texas in the ship and they got off, he was going into town to buy all this stuff. Because of rationing in Great Britain, he was buying clothes for the family. He got on the wrong side of the bus and the bus driver wouldn't move because of segregation. I said, "What self-respecting black man wants to be sitting beside you, dad?"'

Mavis met a lot of family resistance. Her father tried to talk her out of marriage, even making a last appeal on her wedding day in 1945. Firstly, he was 'a bit of a lefty'. Also, the surname Hooley was an issue. The hooligan was associated with stage-Irish characters

33

George Hooley

advice on housing and employment issues. In 1948, Mavis was pregnant again and missing home. So she returned to Belfast alone.

'This was something that women really didn't do in those days – she got up and came back. She wanted to be with her big family. And I really admire my mother for doing that.'

Terence Wilfred Hooley was born at his grandfather's place on Cameron Street on 23 December 1948 ('There were three stars in the heavens above the house. If you believe that, you'll believe anything.'). His uncle Wilf had fetched the doctor during a heavy snowfall and so the new child was gifted a middle name in his honour.

George Hooley came back to Belfast when he had arranged the handover with a new councillor. His new

in music hall and satirical English and American sketches. This was possibly derived from the historic name Ó hUalacháin, which had links to the High Kings, derived from the Irish word uallach, meaning 'proud'. Meantime, a 'hooley' carried the threat of parties and riotous behaviour.

'My grandfather said to my mum one day, "How am I gonna get Terri into the Junior Orange Order with a name like Hooley?" And my mum says, "You won't, because he's not joining. And he'll make up his own mind when he's older." Later, my grandfather cried for weeks when he saw me in the march against the banning of the Republican Clubs (in 1967). I was going to him, "Times are changing – this is like the Nazis, you just can't go banning political parties".'

Mavis and George Hooley married and moved to Leek, Staffordshire, where their first son John was born. In 1947, George was elected as a Labour Party councillor. It was a demanding role and people would queue up at the house in the evenings, looking for

POLLING DAY
21st MAY, 1952
BETWEEN
8.30 a.m. & 8.30 p.m.

YOU VOTE AT
LOMOND AVE. SCHOOL.

PLEASE VOTE THUS
FOR ALDERMAN

| PURDY, W. D. | X |

FOR COUNCILLOR

BELL, H. A. K.	X
HOOLEY, G.	X
O'DOGHERTY. C. B.	X

34

challenge was to find employment and to apply his socialist principles in a city that was mostly enforced along sectarian lines.

'My grandfather said, "I don't know how we're going to get you a job with my Orange Order connections" and my dad says, "Stuff your Orange Order connections, I'm going to get my own job". So my dad got a job in the Post Office Engineering Union. And he was at one of the meetings and he was asking a lot of questions, and they were looking for a new Secretary. So they said, "What about him?" And my father took a job and he ended up on a National Executive Council of the Post Office Engineering Union. And he travelled the world with the union. So he would go away. He came into my life as a stranger and I actually think he left my life as a stranger.'

One of the important dates in the family calendar was May Day – when the unions and the Labour Party paraded. One of the banners the Hooleys carried had a basic demand: 'one man, one vote'. This became a central ask of the civil rights movement in Northern Ireland as the protests became more insistent from 1968 onwards. Another significant day in the year was Remembrance Sunday, on which George Hooley laid a wreath on behalf of the Post Office Engineering Union.

'So my politics really started when I was young. My mother was very Christian and my father wasn't Christian at all. He'd seen enough stuff in the war not to believe in it. I was brought up as a Christian by my mother, and sort of socialist by my father. Somewhere in the middle, I thought that they met. There wasn't much of a difference.

'There was a lot of discrimination against Catholics, which really, really upset me. Because I was brought up to believe that we're all a family of man – I've got a brother in Melbourne, a sister in Paris and the whole wide world was mom and dad to me, and we're all here to look after each other. I never actually knew, until later on, that my father was Church of England. I didn't know if he was Catholic or Protestant. It wasn't important in our house.'

His mother walked in support of the rent strikes. George was the first person to sing the socialist anthem 'The Red Flag' in Belfast's City Hall, at a Labour and Trade Union conference. 'And the unionists wanted him banned. They wanted to ban the trade unions from ever using the city hall again.' The family wouldn't buy Spanish goods because of Franco's Fascist regime. They boycotted South African products, protesting at the system of apartheid.

George Hooley stood for election several times in east Belfast. He was often abused and even attacked on the street. 'We were in Garnerville. My dad had been beaten up the night before – he'd been bricked. My mum went down to the corner shop. And they came round to our house. We were in bed. They came round to our house with their bands. We went out to the window to wave to them. Next thing, they started throwing things at the house and shouting, "Go back

George with the Leek Youth Circle Jazz Band

John, Mavis and Terri

George Hooley (third left), May Day, Belfast, 1971. Image by Bill Kirk.

to Cork, you Fenian bastards!" And I just realised, "These people are nuts". Everybody knew my dad was from England.

'My dad was in many ways badly treated, even though he was English. And yet my dad had a fantastic garden. People used to go, "Oh, Mr Hooley, I forgot to get a lettuce". He'd give them a lettuce and he never charged them. But they'd never vote for him. He seemed to be feeding half the street.'

In 1954, the family lived in a pre-fabricated bungalow in Glenluce Drive in the Garnerville estate. But when Terri lost his eye, Mavis contacted a unionist councillor on the Lisburn Road, who helped the family to move to a new home, 12 Hillfoot Street. 'We got a brand new house. I don't know how my dad felt about that. I talk about the day that we could afford lino for the bathroom. We had a party with tea and buns. We thought we'd made it. Hillfoot Street was my world.'

His brother John started dressing in the Edwardian style, the Teddy boy subculture that coincided with the arrival of rock and roll. 'They were the first people who didn't wear the cloth caps and stuff like that, like our fathers and our grandfathers had.' Yet the Hooley sons were not compatible. John even hid Terri's glass eye. He kept it for a couple of days for no reason other than malice.

'My brother was a nasty bastard. My mum aways said that if I was in the garden, happy, playing with a stone, he had to have that stone. My brother stole something from the house and my dad accused me and my dad beat me up. And then my brother came home and he admitted it. I'd been sent to bed. And I remember my mum came up and gave me a chocolate biscuit. But my dad never apologised for that. My father was very hard on me. I often feel that he thought I spoilt his political career because he moved here.'

Terri and John were estranged when the brother died. There had been many disagreements about his personal affairs, lifestyle and his hard drug use that had caused stresses in the family.

'One time, I went back to the house and my dad went, "The head of the drugs squad was on the phone, looking for you". Dad got stuck into me. I said to him, "Oh, by the way, it's not me they're after, it's your favourite son – he's been busted and in jail and I've sent Pat (his wife) money and she's moved back home, to Liverpool, to be with her family". He just took that really bad. I don't think he ever forgave me for saying that.

'When he died, this was all my father ever said about him. He said, "If you and your mum are going to his funeral, don't take any Northern Ireland notes with you (to Hebden Bridge), 'cos they won't take them in the pub". He never really mentioned him again. That was it. I think he realised in the end that he'd backed the wrong horse.'

The Miseducation of
Terence Hooley

Terri was six when he got his first record. He kept it hidden in the airing cupboard. It was a flexidisc, given away free to promote Summer County margarine. Even though the delivery guy had put a copy though the letterbox of 22 Dunluce Drive, Terri knew that his brother would claim ownership, so he ran down the road and begged the man for a second record, for himself.

The artist was Humphrey Lyttelton, the trumpet player and bandleader who had brought British jazz into the charts in 1956 with 'Bad Penny Blues'. By the time he had signed the margarine deal, Humph was broadening his act and taking on media commissions. Terri didn't know any of that. He didn't even have a record player at the time. Yet when he fetched the record out of its hiding place, he was enthralled by the words, the groove and the secret codes. The

Terri outside City Hall, Belfast

music was thinly pressed on one side of the plastic – he called it a 'flip-flop' record. There was an original track called 'Swingin' on the Gate', followed by a version of the Stephen Foster tune 'Jeanie with the Light Brown Hair'.

Before he could actually hear it, Terri created games around the lettering on the record sleeve. He would take the names of friends and see how many letters matched with the text on the flexidisc package. He awarded points and created championships. The record had the power to make this happen. It was a

source of divination, the all-knowing I Ching that he kept safe under the blankets and bed linen.

A friend called Tommy asked him for help, shifting some furniture to an aunt's house, ready for a wedding party. She had a record player and so Terri got his chance to experience the record's actual music after this suspenseful build-up. 'When I heard it for the first time I thought, "Jesus, this is just wonderful".'

He heard music when his dad sat by the radio for *Two Way Family Favourites* and the Sunday service.

Terri attended Baptist Hall meetings, especially for the tunes and the tambourines. When they tried to save his soul, he was less receptive. 'No, just totally here for the music,' he said, and never returned.

George came home from a union visit to Sweden with a transistor radio, which meant his son could listen on the move, searching the dial for the Voice of America station and Radio Luxembourg. Previously, there had been a crystal set receiver that used his metal bedframe as an aerial. His self-sufficiency in music was complete when he got a Dansette record player from the Kay's mail-order catalogue. The weekly installments were a shilling and sixpence. A decent investment.

In 1966, he took a photograph of his growing record collection, arranged on his bed in Hillfoot Street. This was his life, happily resounding to The Rolling Stones, The Kinks, The Yardbirds and The Animals. An album by Chuck Berry followed the origins of the UK R&B boom back to America while the first EP by Them was proof that the music was also enthralling Belfast. There were maverick choices from Andrew Loog Oldham plus ballads from Sandie Shaw and Petula Clark. French pop and the arrival of winsome yé-yé ballads had reached Terri's collection with Françoise Hardy and 'On se Plaît'. Love, she sang, was perfect for the now, but it might not last forever.

In his early teens, he selected the discs at the church youth club in Strand Presbyterian at Connsbrook Avenue. By 1965, he was headed along the coast of Belfast Lough, destination Holywood and Bangor.

'The band would be playing a gig, maybe in Holywood, and I would get on the train with my Dansette and my records. I'd use the band's PA and put the microphone in front of the speaker of the record player. I remember having to buy a universal plug, 'cos in those days, some of the halls had 15 amp plugs or 5 amp plugs and then some had 13 amps. You had to get a universal plug and fiddle about with it. It was good fun. And while I was changing the records on the Dansette, I would do a bit of talking between the records, which I was never really fond of.

'Photography and music were my two big loves. When I started going out with girls, I kind of gave up on the photography. And then my first job was at Erskine Mayne's – photo printing at the side of the City Hall, in the basement. This was right beside the record department. And the reps used to come in on a Friday and they would be playing all the new releases and I was always really interested. And the reps would say, "Terri, do you want these records?"

I was just so grateful. It was brilliant. So then I used to have 'Terri's Tip For The Top'. It was a record that people had maybe never heard of. The first one was 'When a Man Loves a Woman' by Percy Sledge.'

Another one of his early 1966 selections was 'River Deep, Mountain High', by Ike and Tina Turner, intensely produced by Phil Spector. It seemed that Terri had an ear for the 60s pop gestalt. 'People used to wonder what my tip would be, which surprised me.' He was billed on the posters outside his regular gigs at the King Edward Hall in Holywood and was a feature at the Scout Hall in Bangor's Ward Park, just beside the Duck Pond.

'There were a lot of bands playing in the Co-op hall in Bangor. They had 'Belfast's number one DJ, Terri Hooley' on the poster. I was taking one of the posters down and this big policeman came over and said, "What are you doing there, son?" I said, "I'm taking this poster home to show my mother". And he went, "Oh, here's a better one", and he took it down for me. But I think the bands had put that up as a joke.'

His schooling at Ashfield Boys had not been memorable.

'I had no interest in school at all. I'd be looking out the window thinking about John Leyton singing 'Johnny Remember Me'. And Carole King singing 'It Might as Well Rain Until September'. I had no fucking interest in school and I hated the teachers. People talk about the Christian Brothers, but they had nothing on our teachers. Ashfield was one of the hardest schools in Belfast.

'I suffered from migraine headaches when I was at school. I wasn't allowed to do sports or anything. I used to do cross country running on a Saturday morning. The loneliness of the long-distance runner – that was me!'

And then the most extraordinary thing happened. Terri was basically adopted by three grammar schoolgirls, who saw his potential and decided to give him an artistic and social education. It was a like George Bernard Shaw's *Pygmalion*, with Terri as Eliza Doolittle. Meantime, the Henry Higgins part of mentoring and upskilling was the combined work of Doreen Hewitt, Valerie Hewitt and Pauline Harrison.

As with many of Terri's stories, there's a vivid preamble. It begins in 1965, outside Jack Sinclair's Newsagents, 58 Upper Newtownards Road, Belfast. Terri and his friend Tommy Lyttle noticed a girl called Maureen at the bus stop, headed out of town.

'Tommy says to me, "Have you seen that girl standing at the bus stop? She's either an actress or a model or something." I says, "I might only have one eye, but I certainly see her". So we went and looked in Sinclair's shop window at the jars of Dolly Mixtures and Brandy Balls and stuff. We were looking at her and he says, "I dare you to go and ask her out".

'I was very young, and she was a lot older. And I went over to her, and I says, "Excuse me miss, my name's Terri. My mate and I were just saying how beautiful you were. And he's dared me to ask you out. So would you talk to me a minute and then I'll leave you alone?"

'And she says, "You think I'm good looking?" I says, "You're the most beautiful girl I've ever seen".

'She says, "I'm getting the bus up to Dundonald to see a guy and I don't think we really get on that well". I says, "Well, if it was me I'd be getting the bus down to see you". She says, "I tell you what, if it doesn't work out well tonight I'll be at the Belmont Tennis Club dance on Saturday night".'

He was on half a promise, so the next evening, Terri borrowed his brother's Teddy boy jacket and ironed it. Likewise with his shirt. He had a bath and even though he had no facial hair, he used his father's Gillette razor and finished the ritual off with a splash of the Old Spice aftershave that George's aunt had sent him, which he had never used.

'I was walking past The Strand picture house. They were queuing up. You could have smelt me three streets away. And I thought I was the coolest kid. I paid in to the tennis club. I didn't know that you had to be a member, but they let me in. I think they thought I was care in the community. I was waiting for Maureen to come, and she never turned up. And then these three girls came up to me and said to me, "Are you trying to be a hard man?" I said "No, no. I'm more into the pacifist principles of Gandhi, and all."

'They said, "What the fuck are you doing?" So I told them the story. And they laughed. They said, "Get rid of the jacket and come up and dance". I said, "I can't dance. My dad's a great dancer but I can't." They said, "We'll show you how to dance". I had a dance and stuff and then they said to me, "What are you doing tomorrow?" I said, "Oh, tomorrow afternoon, I'll be listening to the chart show to see if The Animals are number one". They said, "Would you like to meet us for a picnic, in Stormont grounds?"

'So I went up, not expecting them to be there, after my first 'date'. And then they invited me down to this big house down by Massey Avenue. And they asked me what I wanted to drink.

'Cos I had seen the ad, I said, "I'll have a Babycham" and they laughed. Pauline Harrison said, "You're a Guinness and a brandy man". They gave me drink and then this guy gave me a lift home in a green sports car. I thought, "Fuck, I've made it".'

He skipped school the next day because the hangover was severe. He assumed that his association with these libertines was finished.

'One night, I was in my bedroom and my mum said, "There are some lovely girls at the door, wanting to know if you're going out". So I disappeared with them. They led me astray. It's the best education I ever had.'

They gave him books to read. Terri wasn't keen on Friedrich Nietzsche but he liked Stan Barstow, plus *The L-Shaped Room* by Lynne Reid Banks. 'Basically, I read the books that the girls gave me and then we could talk about them. And then they would explain to me what it was all about.'

Another author they got him interested in was J.D. Salinger. He was fine with *The Catcher in the Rye*, but *Raise High the Roof Beam, Carpenters* was a favourite. He especially liked the stories about the fictional Glass family in New York. He loved the part in *Franny and Zooey* when Franny splutters, *'I'm just sick of ego, ego, ego. My own and everybody else's. I'm sick of everybody that wants to get somewhere, do something distinguished and all, be somebody interesting. It's disgusting.'*

This registered with the teenager. 'Well, I was trying to do interesting things. And I developed an ego. Which covered up my deep-rooted inferiority complex. As many people do.'

It was Doreen, Valerie and Pauline who had spotted the job vacancy at W. Erskine Mayne and put in a word for him. They escorted him to folk clubs and exhibitions and found him DJ bookings in North Down.

'They took me into my first bar in Queen's Arcade. And the barman says, "Is he old enough to drink?" And Doreen just said, "He's with us, he's old enough". They introduced me to all these people – people out of bands. It was just wonderful. Took me to art gallery openings. It was a whole different world.'

Terri took time off school, telling the teachers that he had to get his eye examined at the Royal Hospital. He was really headed to the Friday lunchtime sessions at The Plaza, where they had a revolving stage. Doreen would call into a businessman's club above the Garrick Bar on Chichester Street. 'She'd say, "Dad, give us some money", and then she'd give it to me.'

Terri was perhaps a kind of a project, a plan to subvert the class barriers.

'I think I was like a project. I think I amused them. And I think I was different from all the Campbell College boys. They hated them. And they really liked me. I was very attracted to the counterculture. I liked beatnik girls. My life changed, definitely. I was certainly a lot happier. They were taking me to things that I didn't know existed.'

He visited their family homes in the affluent Belmont area of east Belfast and enjoyed the parents' record collections. It was a proper introduction to Charlie Parker, Nina Simone and Ella Fitzgerald. Even some Paganini. 'I just wanted to hear everything. They were going, "Stick on The Kinks..." or The Stones or The Beatles. They were all big Beatles fans and I was more into The Stones.' Indeed, Terri had seen the band at the Ulster Hall in September 1965 and Mick Jagger had bought him a Coke afterwards at the Central Hotel.

He was also reading beat literature like William Burroughs and Jack Kerouac. It was decades later when he finally made it to San Francisco and paid his dues to the City Lights bookstore from which the beats had propagated. He went to the nearby Vesuvio Bar, another famous haunt. He ordered Guinness and brandy, just as the Strathearn girls had taught him to. And he toasted the poets, like Lawrence Ferlinghetti, Allen Ginsberg and Gregory Corso. San Francisco was a bit of a disappointment in the 21st Century, but the road that had taken him there was astonishing.

Past,
Present
& Future

I n 1966, trouble was imminent. It was the 50th anniversary of the Easter Rising, a major event in the Irish republican story. It was also the 10th anniversary of the IRA border campaign, commemorated in popular songs like 'Seán South of Garryowen' and 'The Patriot Game'. On the other side, a paramilitary group had reclaimed the name of the Ulster Volunteer Force and was threatening to execute IRA combatants. Meantime, Ian Paisley was leading the Free Presbyterians and other fundamentalists to protest against liberal politics and an ecumenical drift in the North.

On 6 June, Paisley's followers marched through Belfast and then picketed the Presbyterian Church in Ireland's General Assembly at Howard Street in Belfast. It was a fractious, provocative day and Paisley was imprisoned for his involvement and his refusal to comply. In July, the government of Northern Ireland decided that it should act decisively and quell the street unrest.

It pulled together parts of the Special Powers Acts and the Public Order Act. It banned processions and unapproved public meetings in Belfast for three months. It adapted the Special Powers legislation with the aim to disperse any assembly of three or more persons wherever there was reasonable belief that the assembly might lead to a breach of the peace. Failing to disperse, when asked to, would be an offence.

So, Terri Hooley and his mates decided they were still going to block Wellington Place, near the city hall. He was 17 and he was Chairman of the Northern Ireland Youth Campaign for Peace and Nuclear Disarmament. For this seditious act, Terri and his accomplice Paul Murphy were the first two people arrested under the new provisions. Murphy had been playing 'We Shall Not Be Moved' on his guitar when they took them away.

Hooley attended the court hearing but confusion followed.

'This policeman came in, looking for change for the phone. I said, "I have some change".

'He says to me, "Don't tell me you're married, son?" I says, "Not likely". He said, "What are you doing

Backstage at the McMordie Hall, Belfast

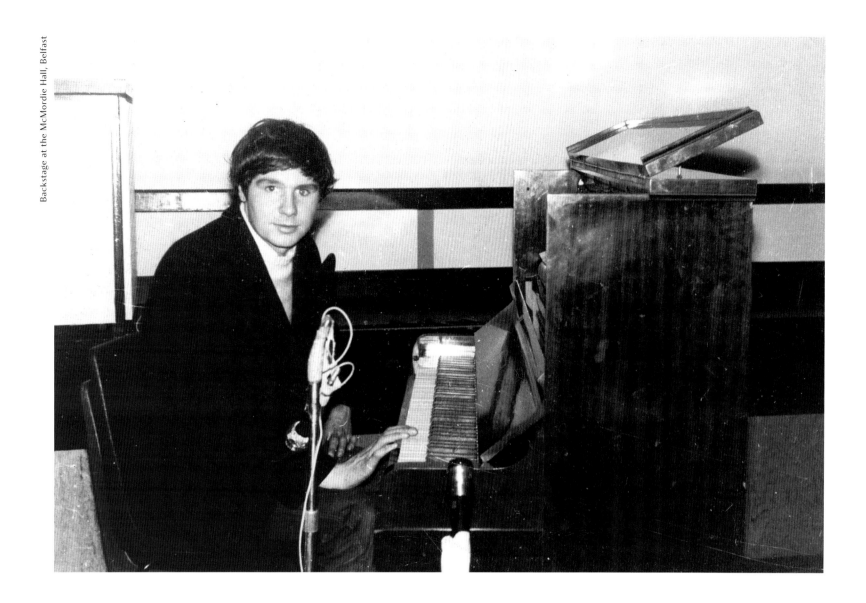

here?" I said, "I'm here because I believe in the fight for the abolishment of nuclear weapons and the preservation of humanity and an end to the war of aggression on the men, women and children of Vietnam – dropping their Lazy Dog missiles and their napalm bombs."

'He said, "You're in the wrong court, son. This is the Maintenance Court." So, I went down to the other court and apparently everybody thought that I hadn't turned up as a protest. I got fined £20.'

His friends Valerie Hewitt and Pauline Harrison paid the fine and Terri's reputation as a street activist was enhanced. That said, he was disappointed. 'I was prepared to write my prison letters.'

He had found his own political focus after the Cuban Missile Crisis of 1962, when a nuclear showdown between America and Russia had seemed likely. He signed up for the ideals of the Campaign for Nuclear Disarmament (CND) and tried to stage a coup with his local branch when he supposed that they were overly fond of pints in the Duke of York. He brought his mates down to the Maritime Jazz Club to sway the vote, but the CND guys had batted him away on issues of governance and so he formed his own breakaway group, the NIYCPND. They announced a protest march from Belfast to Bangor but in truth, many of them took the train.

He was also chairman of the Belfast Council for Peace in Vietnam.

'My revolution was never about killing my brothers and sisters because of an accident of birth or religion. I was never really interested in Northern Ireland politics. I was interested in what was happening in Vietnam, Cambodia, Chile and Latin America.

'It was a growing realisation. I just didn't trust the Americans as the policemen of the world. I thought they were basically propping up a corrupt regime in the south of Vietnam. What was going on was terrible. I just felt that I couldn't sit back and say nothing. So we used to have meetings and then our meetings were banned outside the City Hall.

'I was allowed to have two people holding a banner saying, 'Remember Hiroshima' (on 6 August). We used to get attacked by the Free Presbyterians. I really did think we could change the world. I was very much interested in the Civil Rights movement in America and singers like Nina Simone.'

Terry Hooley—leader of two young pacifist bodies in Belfast, claims that Belfast people have no interest in the Vietnam War.

Belfast folk not interested in 'peace'?

the military-industrial complex. But in 1966, Dylan was backing away from the absolute declarations of protest music and began writing lyrics that were brilliantly strange. The new music was also amplified, upsetting the folk crowd even more. This rowdy carnival arrived at the ABC Theatre, Belfast on 6 May 1966. Dylan and The Band. They brought the promise of an acoustic set at the beginning and then the raging, electric show, ending with 'Like a Rolling Stone'. Terri was outside with a placard, protesting.

He was brought into the venue for a brief moment and Hooley confronted Dylan. He wanted to know why the singer wasn't withholding his taxes, taking his nation to account over the Vietnam war. Other artists, such as Joan Baez, were doing exactly this. Why not Bob? In response, the artist told Terri to 'Fuck off'.

There was dissenting music in the air from Phil Ochs, who had released an album of protest anthems, *I Ain't Marching Any More*, in 1965. Joan Baez was part of the youth soundtrack and Terri was fond of the Judy Collins recording of 'Marat/Sade', taken from the stage musical about the French Revolution. She sang about bloody regime change and retribution. The aristocrats, the King, the generals – they all had to go:

Marat, we're poor

And the poor stay poor

Marat, don't make us wait any more

We want our rights and we don't care how

We want a revolution now.

Bob Dylan had become a figurehead, visible on the freedom drives, the voter registration events, singing about racist murders and upholding the rebellious tradition of Woody Guthrie and Pete Seeger. Terri was especially fond of 'Masters of War', a takedown of

One of Terri's school acquaintances was Ronnie Bunting. He was the son of Major Bunting, a former army officer and Paisley supporter whose method was to harry the civil rights marches with his militia group the Loyal Citizens of Ulster. But the son was on a different, left-leaning steer. He eventually co-founded the Irish Republican Socialist Party and the Irish National Liberation Army.

'Ronnie and I would be on the same demonstrations. Like, we were both members of the Irish-Arab Friendship Society and we'd be out demonstrating against what was happening in Palestine and people like that. And I got to know a lot of people on the left in those days, and a lot of people who later became involved in the civil rights, and then a lot of people who later joined organisations like the IRA.

'I hired out a room from the World Socialist Party (53 High Street). There were four of them - two were ex-IRA men from the 50s campaign. And they wanted the wageless, moneyless, classless society. I had marched, pre the civil rights, against the banning

of the Republican Clubs, with a lot of friends like Joe Mulheron and Brian Moore, who later became The Men of No Property, singing modern republican songs. In the school that I came up with, I was a bit out of place. A lot of people didn't like me because of my politics.'

For a short time, counterculture was flourishing in Belfast.

'There were 80 clubs in or around Belfast where you could go to hear music. The town was buzzing. We were talking about freedom of thought, action and expression. On a Sunday night, you used to get 1,000 people at the City Hall, so they had to open up Donegall Square Methodist Church and let all the people in. The Rev Hedley Plunkett opened it up so that the kids could have tea and coffee They called it Heaven.

'My Friday night would have been going up to the Spanish Rooms on the Falls Road, with three or four mates, and we'd buy a gallon of cider for a pound. And then we would drink that in the entry and get 1/6 back on the container. And then we'd go down to the Maritime (on College Square North) and we'd buy a pound deal of hashish from Joe Yak and we'd smoke that, because there was no drink in the dance halls.

'And then we would hear Van Morrison and Them or The Just Five or The Alleykatz – many, many great bands that were around at that time. And then we got the 11 o'clock bus home. And if you got a kiss and a cuddle from a girl at the bus stop, that was brilliant. And that was a really good night. And then suddenly, things had changed.'

Weldon 'Juke Boy' Bonner was a bluesman from Bellville, Texas. He had been born into a sharecropper family, the youngest of nine children, orphaned at the age of six. He had worked in the fields during the cotton season before moving to Houston as a teenager, keenly learning from the jukebox. On 14 November 1969, he was set to perform at Belfast's War Memorial Building.

The night had been organised by the record shop owner Dougie Knight and the Belfast Blues Society. Terri Hooley was Secretary of the Society. They had put a lot of effort into poster design and promotion and arranged to sell food at the venue to cover some of the costs. Interest in the blues was holding up and there was audience enough during this period for a series of valued guests: Champion Jack Dupree, Memphis Slim and Mississippi Fred McDowell. But it was going to be a challenge for the Juke Boy gig, as Terri remembers:

'That Friday night, because of rioting, all the bars in Belfast city centre closed at teatime. The only place you could get a drink was at our concert on Waring Street.'

They brought the singer in through diversions and around roadblocks. And the night was reasonably well attended. Everyone there had made a personal effort to be present. They were keen to make Juke Boy feel welcome and Terri's friend Pauline got up on stage and kissed the man on the cheek.

Soon after, Juke Boy wrote a song called 'Belfast Blues'. It was a recollection of his evening at the War Memorial Building in a city with a worsening international reputation. The memory was only a few days old, but already he had a theme and a riff. Belfast, he declared in his song, was a surprising place. The men were friendly and the women were sweet and kind. He told his listeners that the city had

Dougie Knight's record shop, 1969

doimissher, justat nightimes. doimissher, justat rightimes. yes i do yes i do yes i do yes i do every minute of the day.

floored him, that a woman had even come up and kissed him on the cheek. He made it sound joyous.

It was a while before the record was released and longer again before Terri got to hear 'Belfast Blues'. By then, the concerts had become less frequent and the city centre was a place of random violence. The song was an emotional keepsake.

'The 60s for me was like a great big party which I thought would never end – but by November 1969 I knew it was over. It was the night we stopped partying. A lot of the people who had gone to places like the Jazz Club and the Maritime went back to their own ghettoes and people lost contact with each other. And we were going into a horrific part of history in Northern Ireland. That was the night when the kissing had to stop.'

Terri's elegy for the decade was a Shangri-Las' track, 'Past, Present & Future'. A song about damage and sorrow, set to the melody of Beethoven's *Moonlight Sonata*. There was a brief, sad waltz in the middle of the recording. Everything about the record was beautifully wracked.

The Shangri-Las had started with Mary and her sister Betty, plus the twins Marge and Mary Ann Ganser. Raised in Cambria Heights, a rough neighbourhood in Queens, New York, they had big hair and lashes. They wore leather and sang tragic songs about delinquent boys. They were good-bad but not evil.

As with many of their songs, an awful event had taken place – something from which the lover was unlikely to recover. This was a fashionable theme in 60s pop, repeated in records from the likes of Jan and Dean, John Leyton and Roy Orbison. 'Past, Present & Future' is sketchy with the detail but the listener realises that here is a tragic aftermath. Love may not ever happen again.

Terri's first girlfriend, Doreen, had been killed in a car accident on the way back from a night in Bangor. He had decided not to attend the party, as he was out painting anti-Vietnam slogans around Belfast. He had known Doreen for 18 months. Afterwards, he played the Shangri-Las record often.

'I used to sit in the bedroom; I just thought I'd never be with anybody again. My mom used to hear me crying in bed at night. I used to sit in bed, and I'd play this. I was quite a lonely kid.

I would say that's a very personal record for me, and it's part of my growing up.'

The Ego
Has Landed

I

n 1969, Ruth Carr was moving from Ballysillan in north Belfast to Botanic Avenue by Queen's University. She was at the start of a writing career and felt that the restless mood in the city might be a throwback to the days of 1798.

'It was a bit like the United Irishmen time. All these ideas were flooding in from elsewhere, that make you think, "Oh, the world doesn't have to be the way it seems to be here". You're looking at anti-war, anti-racism, Vietnam, CND. In 1969, my brother was at Queen's and because of everything that happened, there was a curfew. You were banned from meeting more than three people in the street. I was just a kid running around with flowers on my face. We were all laughing, saying we were gonna get arrested.

'A lot of people were waking up to a kind of idealism that was sort of floating around. As if we could be something. I was very influenced by ideas. Peace and

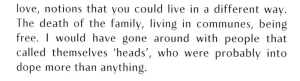

love, notions that you could live in a different way. The death of the family, living in communes, being free. I would have gone around with people that called themselves 'heads', who were probably into dope more than anything.

'Then of course everything happened, and the army came in and internment and everything. I think that's why I mentioned the United Irishmen – because there was this beautiful idea and it was such anathema to the status quo. And the status quo just crushed it. It wrecked people's lives. To me, that's what happened. The people who suffered internment and the people whose houses were smashed up by house searches, and plastic bullets – that was just horrible.

'I think that's why Terri went into the music and that why I was involved with Terri, because we found we were in the same neck of the woods, you know, that all that stuff is a load of shit. It's soft politics if you like. You don't want to get involved with guns, you

Selling ID magazine at Donegall Place, Belfast

John Gilbert

don't believe in those causes, really, but at the same time you want to assert something that you feel is worthwhile and matters. And music was a voice in that way. Most people that we knew were escaping from the labels that were on the outside. Or the way you were always labelled here.'

Terri also recalls the escalating violence.

'The thing that shocked me at the time – because we were all going to these clubs and having a great time and all hanging about together – was how quickly my city became divided. And that came as a big shock to me and how quickly people got involved in the paramilitaries. It must have been under the surface, a lot of it. But which I hadn't seen. But people very quickly took sides. And then was a whole lot of us that decided that we weren't going to take sides and we were called The Tribe and we set up underground magazines and we tried to keep everybody together.

'Even they left Northern Ireland, either because the police harassment or harassment from the paramilitaries and stuff. And I made a conscious decision that I was going to stay in Belfast and not to take sides. I'm very proud of the fact that I never took sides and it never went out and I never killed anybody, but a lot of my friends did.

'A lot of my friends ended up in jail. And there's a lot of a lot of people who have had friends whose brothers were very quiet – never seemed to leave the house – turned out to be mad bombers. And things were very difficult. But it really did come as a shock to me how quickly Belfast became divided. How quickly it became ghettoised. And there was a big displacement of population. I think it was bigger than anywhere else since the Second World War. And the town just became so divided.'

The first issue of *ID* magazine, edited by Terri in 1970, imagined this free-thinking community on page three. The dedication list includes over 200 names – the poets, agitators, strummers and dreamers. It included Van Morrison and Seamus Heaney, plus Geraldine Lynne, founder of the Fresh Garbage emporium on

Bank Street, and the painter Neil Shawcross. The remit was alternative verse and visuals and Terri sold it in town, outside the City Hall.

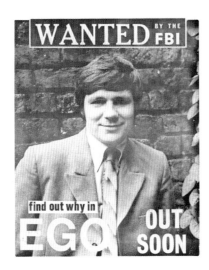

A second publication, *Ego*, was launched in July 1970, this time a newspaper with a cover price of 6d. '*Ego* belongs to you, the progressive-minded youth of today,' he wrote. He printed up 1,200 copies and he claimed that he sold 800 on the streets within a few days. Coming issues gave space to the Gay Liberation Front, astrology and the Divine Light Mission. Later, there were a couple of free editions of *A Breath of Fresh Air,* again celebrating the counterculture.

Terri planned to use the magazine proceeds to create a 'Bust Fund' with information sheets for those arrested for drugs misdemeanours, similar to the Release organisation in London. 'The police say they have 1,700 names in their drug users' files,' he figured. 'I hope they have a few interesting things in my file as some of the stories I have been told about this Terri Hooley bloke are quite unbelievable.' This aim was realised with *The Belfast Index* – an alternative guide to community action, helplines, hostels and voluntary groups.

He made a formal declaration about his new community – The Tribe – in *City Week*, 1 October 1970. They were planning to raise £1,000 to create the Belfast Arts Lab (BAL), possibly incorporating an independent press, poster workshop and a head shop. There was also going to be a record release, a split single featuring his friend John B plus Ed Emmett, the folk-blues guitarist. To illustrate the potential of his plans, Terri offered some poetry:

'BAL is a phone call.

BAL is in the mind.

BAL is not LAL.

BAL is BAL is BAL.

BAL is you being you...'

In the same *City Week* feature, Terri took the journalist to a derelict building on the Oldpark Road. This northside wreck was a potential site for BAL, he enthused. The locals were less approving and a restless mob gathered outside. The police arrived in a Land Rover, confiscated the photographer's film and demanded identification from Hooley. This tense scenario resulted in a rethink. 'I might have to try somewhere else,' he mused. Only later did Terri reveal that he had been under the influence of LSD during his Oldpark visit.

Free radio was another of his ambitions. 'If we start talking about love, peace and happiness on the air,' he imagined, 'the powers that be would more than likely jam the frequency.' So, in the early months of 1971, he and Tommy Little were broadcasting from an abandoned house on the Rocky Road, high up in the Castlereagh Hills. During one pirate session, an army patrol arrived at the door. Tommy had been playing 'Alone Again Or' by Love and was rigid with anxiety, but the squaddies were only looking for directions. Radio Harmony persisted.

The pair of them went to London to search out radio equipment and fetched up at a party on the Portobello Road. John Lennon was there, but masses of dope had been consumed and recollections were hazy afterwards. However, they did visit a lock-up garage, possibly in the Highbury area. Terri was confounded. 'Lennon was completely off his rocker. One of his friends took us to the garage and showed us these boxes of rifles and wanted to know how we could get them back to Northern Ireland. I said, "We're the boys, but we're not those boys..."'

Next day there was a meeting with some of the *Oz* people and a party in a well-heeled part of the city. Lennon was there again and words were spoken, as Hooley remembers. 'The discussion turned to Northern Ireland and Lennon started spouting what I can only describe as green, nationalist, graveyard shit. We began to argue, it got nasty and I ended up swinging for him.' In another account, Terri recalled the final confrontation being outside. 'We had a big row in a graveyard and John beat me up in the end. He could fight better than me.'

The guitarist Rory Gallagher was booked to play the Ulster Hall on New Year's Day 1972. He was one of the few top-tier musicians who stayed loyal to Belfast during the worst times. On the night before the show, ten bombs had been detonated, a statement of intent from the IRA. Outside the venue, Terri Hooley's friends from The Tribe had been leafleting with a newsletter, *Take One*, and a new cause, the Music to

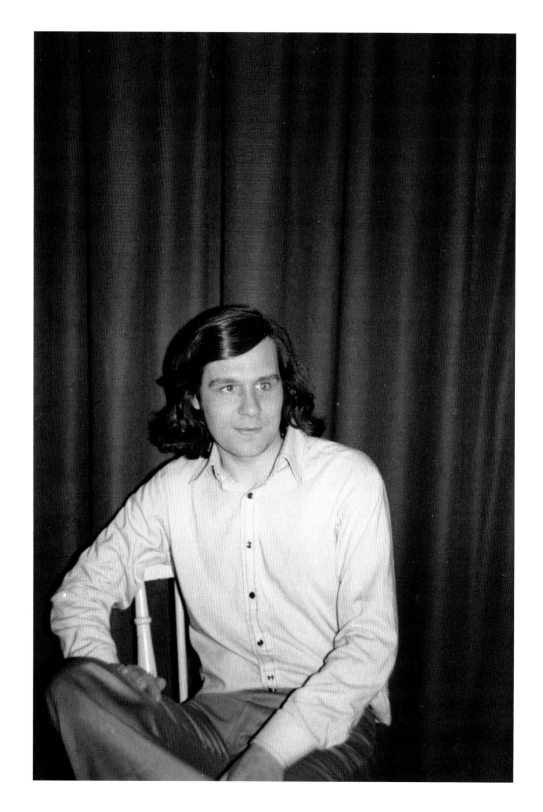

Belfast Campaign. They talked to the journalist from *Melody Maker*. They said were proud of Rory but unimpressed by the timidity of the music industry.

'Belfast has now become a graveyard for music,' The Tribe declared in *Take One*. 'We must create enough noise in order that the hypocrites in England (the capitalist agents who think nothing other than pulling in a lot of bread) become aware that they are most needed in this torn city. We want action now, for too long the groups in England haven't given music where it can give the most help. Lennon tells us to give peace a chance, but has he visited us? All we want John, baby, is the truth. Perhaps he is furthering the peace movements somewhere in Hyde Park.'

1972 was the worst year of the conflict. There were 500 deaths, 2,000 explosions and 10,000 shooting incidents. In July alone, there were 100 deaths.

'The 70s were horrific. You were afraid to go out. There were times when I said goodnight to people and never saw them again. I lost a lot of friends. The country was having a nervous breakdown and everyone was living in fear.'

David Hyndman worked as a compositor at the Northern Whig building in the city centre. He helped with some of Terri's printing projects before they began plotting about bold, community visions. This was another energy source, as Ruth recalls:

'I met Dave Hyndman and Marilyn. She was completely different with red hair. I was just floating around in this area ... of people. The Cooke Street crowd were Dave and Marilyn and Brian Green. They lived in Cooke Street, a collective. They were political and idealistic. Dave called himself The Man in Black. There were all into their ideas of how to run things in a different way.'

Terri and the Print Workshop people at 28 Cooke Street had spent several years with an abstract idea called the Co-operative Craft and Cultural Society Ltd. Richard Watters, who was already running Sassafras Wholefoods on the Donegal Road, was also a partner. They were aiming for funding and looked seriously at a property on 12 Lower Crescent. Their plans had included a restaurant and community TV business, but funders (including the Peace People) were not convinced.

Meantime, Hooley worked in the processing department of McGuinness & Walton, a subsidiary of Kodak, on Corporation Street. One of his tasks was to create funeral mass cards from the photographs of the departed. Sometimes he was asked to process film that had been smuggled out of an internment block. Terri himself had become a potential target when he wouldn't go along with the Ulster Workers' Council Strike in May 1974, a unionist bid to wreck the power-sharing assembly, outlined by the Sunningdale Agreement. His boss created a pretext to take him away to Blackpool on business.

Like many citizens, he was losing his own friends in the conflict and two of them died horrendously in 1974. Gerard McWilliams had been living in England for six years and was only back a few days when he decided to walk home to Andersonstown after a night in Lavery's Bar. They found his body on the morning of 26 September off the Donegall Road. He'd been stabbed and beaten with a blunt instrument. He was 25. Another good soul, Ivan Clayton, had been working on the door of the Club Bar on University Road when he was shot in the stomach by two UDA men who ran off into Sandy Row.

Terri started to write a rock opera called *Bang, Bang, You're Dead*. It was about a gunman who was worshiped like a glam rocker. He would come onstage and outline his working method.

'I don't like the colour of your hair.

Bang, bang, you're dead.

I don't like the clothes you wear.

Bang, bang, you're dead.'

'I told the guys in work about this. I said, "If this musical goes on, I'm gonna invite all the politicians and throw buckets of blood all over them". Then the guys at work would come in and tell me the sickest things to have in the musical. And then I thought, "This is just too sick. I can't continue with it."'

A workmate called Andy was a regular reader of *Exchange and Mart* and he showed an advertisement to Terri. A vendor in England was selling 1,000 singles for £40. Hooley borrowed the money from Ruth (they had married on 24 June 1974) and the sale revealed some valuable stock. He was selling from his house and then put out his stall at markets in Belfast and Ballymena.

This new career was almost obliterated in 1976 by a murder attempt when several gunmen tried to bundle him into a car as he left work at Corporation Street.

'That night I came out of work it was a dark night. I was thinking about going to the pub or something and these three guys jumped out of a car with shooters

and tried to grab me in the car. They knew who I was. This guy, he put the gun at my head and then I grabbed it away and kicked him in the balls. And then the other two were beating me with guns and these docker guys jumped in and saved my life.'

The rescue was another example of Terri's far-reaching matrix. He had known the dockers who saved him because he had helped to re-publish *Idle Hours*, a pamphlet of working-class Belfast poetry from the 30s. He had put it out through an imprint, Eye Publications. Hooley was doing the work as a favour for an anarchist friend, Michael Hall, the nephew of the *Idle Hours* poet, Robert Atkinson. The pair of dockers who had fought off the gunmen had been selling the pamphlet to their mates on the waterfront, but they had barely acknowledged Terri, and he had guessed that they didn't like him.

'I went down to Muldoon's pub next week and I said, "I want to buy them a drink". He says, "What the fuck's wrong with him?" The barman says, "Terri, you're lucky, he really likes you".'

But he was sick afterwards, and visited his doctor for help. Dr John 'Jack' Melotte was a classic family GP, with a surgery on the Woodstock Road.

'I wasn't going into work. I needed a line and I went in on the Monday morning. Jack was a great talker. He asked you about your family and he knew about them. I was the first in. He says, "Terri, you're looking awful well". I said to him, "I'm suffering badly, my migraines are back". I didn't want to say to him (that) three gunmen had just tried to grab me in a car and I'm shiteing myself.

'"Fuck your migraines",' he said to me. "I didn't leave the Parador (bar) until 6 o'clock this morning. Would you run over to the chemists and get us some Alka-Seltzer?" He said, "You're partying too much. If you don't stop taking drugs and drink and partying, you're never going to live till you're 30."'

Terri decided not to slacken up on the mischief. He figured that in the blood-lust of 70s Belfast, he might only have months before another murder bid. 'I decided that I'll just have to go out and party and live life because I could be dead tomorrow.'

if
your
true-self
is honest you
live with your-self
but if everyone around
you is dishonest can you
afford to live with the truth.
lets hope you never put-down anyone who is honest and true again.
I'm
sick
of you
animals
telling me to
be something I
am not. you say its
for my own good. but
won't say why you want
to kill me

TERRI HOOLEY.

Dave Hyndman

I first cooperated with Terri on the *ID* and the *Ego* magazines. I thought I could help out, so I met Terri and I started to design and print and write for the magazine. What I used to do is a sort of 'homer' in the Northern Whig (printers) surreptitiously. It was printed on the sly there. Distribution wasn't huge but I never thought the establishment ever took any notice. You know in Britain, you had a certain things happened (the *Oz* magazine obscenity trial took place at the Old Bailey for six weeks in 1971). But in the north, it was so widespread, so chaotic that a little group of hippies was the least of their problems.

So then we had this idea to start The Belfast Arts Lab. It was in Donegall Street, 'cause we didn't want it anywhere near student land. At that stage, it was quite a big group, and we did get a grant from Community Relations, but then when it came to pay the rent, the Community Relations reneged on their contract. But certain things survived.

Every time I met Terri, I always had to get him up out of bed, always had to make his breakfast. He was pretty bloody awful to work with, trying to get him to do things. But because he had worked on *ID* and *Ego* he had the effect of bringing people together so through Terri, I met some really great people. A few characters who were quite dramatic and dynamic, very thoughtful guys.

I think we realised that Terri was not the force and it all went belly up. We were absolutely living the politics of it' and Terri was friends with a few people in the press and he told them about the arts lab and the press ran this story. He had got the headline on some paper, 'Fun Palace To Open' (the City Week headline was 'Hooley's Folly'). And because we were so sincere, we were absolutely outraged and the more dynamic said, 'this guy has to go - we can't handle this trivial nonsense'. So that was the time when Terri was expelled. But I always kept in contact with Terri he never blamed me for any of it.

After our Arts Lab time, we were all living communally. There were about 10 or 15 people in one house on the Antrim Road, which just happened to be at the top of the New Lodge, so inevitably, the politics of nationalism started to come across and people wanted to engage with that community. Then we moved into a house in south Belfast, where we had a small, offset printing press. It was a great factor

in being able to print your own magazine because the price was prohibitive up to that point. I used to print all the local magazines, where they were all campaigning against redevelopment and all the other social ills of their area. So that's where the Community Press was.

With fanzines and magazines, it was all self-help. I had developed this art box which people could take away and it had the layout and whatever typewriter and everything that they needed to do to create these things. Of course, punks just used to write, which was quite interesting - they're always a challenge to print cos of that and photographing was quite problematic. *Alternative Ulster* was from my memory, the most prolific one. But the rise of punk magazines - that was when Terri started to do his independent stuff. I would print the covers.

Terri had his record shop based in his house at that time. I think he was working for Kodak and was operating pretty low key and had his records in his house. I was always interested in cooperatives and collectives and I thought wouldn't it be good? Because there was another chap, Richard Watters, we knew had started a wholefoods shop called Sassafras just off the entrance to Sandy Row. And I thought if we could combine all these, we could create a kind of momentum of sorts.

So for a long while I kept ringing the landlord up of Great Victoria Street and finally persuaded him to let it out to us. It was me being optimistic about our collective intentions. All the ideologies we had were all about self-management and organising and anti-State. The State was always interested in consolidating its own power and all the rest of it. Anarchism is like 57 varieties of Heinz beans, you've different types, in a way I didn't really try and fixate - I was I suppose,

a bit nerdy. With the fascism of youth, you have a particular outlook on things. But anarchism is such a loose philosophy for a lot of people.

As time wore on, I realised they weren't quite as political as I'd wanted them to be. One of the things I was always interested in was a book shop. You couldn't really get books on politics in Belfast that much, especially the magazines. I remember trying to persuade them that we should have a bookshop in the premises but I don't think they were in favour of that and for good reasons as well I don't think we could have had it big enough, or whatever. So, we found the premises in Winetavern Street (Just Books). We were a group of libertarians / anarchists, but Terri decided that he would run a benefit gig for the book shop. That was the first time I think Undertones played in Belfast (the 'Battle of the Bands' 14 June 1978).

I remember ambling down to the bookshop because I was quite isolated upstairs, working away there, and Terri saying 'listen to this tape'. And he played 'Teenage Kicks' and I said, 'Terri you've got yourself a hit there'. That was the best thing, that was absolutely brilliant. Sadly, he didn't have the resources to really. Typical Terri, just was doing it on a shoestring. I realised there was something that was happening and he'd just be ripped off if there wasn't more thought. And that was paralysing, but there's no chance with Terri and I don't think he'd any chance no matter who it was. Just where he was and the situation.

People have such fond memories of Good Vibes. And of course, there was that rise in independents, people were doing it themselves even outside Terri – I always thought, that's amazing, that's brilliant. Before that. there was the culture of big labels, that was it – if you didn't get a big label, you couldn't get anything made.

Over the
Counter Culture

The plotting became an actuality. The three-storey terrace site at 102 Great Victoria Street was fit for music, words, sedition, community and nourishment. As planned, Richard Watters was on the ground floor with Sassafras Wholefoods. The building was suffused with the smell of his spices and herbs. Dave Hyndman had his print workshop on the top, running off community papers, posters, poetry and fanzines. Terri was in the middle floor with Good Vibrations. He took the name from a Troggs version of the Beach Boys song, which had just been re-issued. Then he appropriated the graphics from the same Troggs release. There was wry humour in the title of the shop: 'It was a joke – we were seriously insane. To call a record shop Good Vibrations in the middle of all that was just bonkers.'

They got a free lease period on the derelict building, put in new windows, fashioned up shop fittings with wood hauled from skips and painted the toilet seat red ('so that it would look nice in case some girls turned up'). Then they had a big party.

It was a mixture of brute will and folly that had brought this endeavour to a street that was landscaped by many explosions. It was said that the Europa was the most bombed hotel in the Western world. Later, that bleak distinction went to the Sarajevo Hilton. The fatality rate for the conflict was approaching 2,000 (about to be referenced in the opening lines of 'Suspect Device' by Stiff Little Fingers). There was a tonnage of British army on the streets and a coiled-up reaction from the locals. People were often jumpy and fearful. Music had the capacity to bring joy and shared lightness but even this was brutalised, notably when three members of The Miami Showband were shot multiple times at point-blank range on their way home from a gig in Banbridge, 31 July 1975. State collusion had caused the deaths of singer Fran O'Toole, trumpeter Brian McCoy and guitarist Tony Geraghty.

Record shops were safe places, resounding with new music and sympathetic company. Good Vibrations was a small location, but it was set out to encourage browsers and a sense of social involvement. And it worked. Great Victoria Street was on the other side of the city centre to Caroline Music on Ann Street, and so music fans created their Saturday afternoon rituals, passing the hours between each shop, stopping at Cornmarket en route, loading up on singles and badges, picture sleeves, fanzines and solidarity. They came on bus rides from Derry, Antrim and Fermanagh.

'The shop was a real meeting place,' says Terri. 'It was like an oasis in the middle of this cultural wasteland. I had to laugh when people later called the area the Golden Mile – there was nothing golden about it. We hadn't a clue what we were doing, really. I was just this mad, ex-hippie.

'We weren't doing fantastically well, but we we're doing okay, better than we thought we would have. And a lot of our ideas – our hippy-dippy ideas – we had to change. Like, one of the ideas I wanted was a place, a seat along the window, where people could sit and have tea and coffee. And all we got was young kids mitching off school and trying to steal everything. So I had to change some of our ideas.'

Still, some of the delinquents brought punk rock energy into the shop. Gordy Owen was a teenager from Sandy Row with bad teeth and a home-made Iggy tattoo on his left hand. He was a punk evangelist and was never at school. Gordy had met the Clash at the cancelled Belfast gig in October '77 and crashed out with them at the Europa Hotel. He used to ring the band at their rehearsal rooms in north London and relay the information to the Belfast faithful. He was also enthusing about a local band called RUDI.

John Carson

Shortly before Good Vibrations opened, The Clash were singing about IRA letter bombs on the lyric of 'Career Opportunities'. In 1976, the Sex Pistols had famously namechecked the paramilitary forces on their first record, 'Anarchy in the UK', taking delight in the notion that England's dreaming was in terminal decline:

Is this the UDA, is this the IRA?

I thought it was the UK.

Or just another country,

Another social tenancy...

Northern Ireland was a rich subject for the confrontational manners and truth-telling of punk rock. Some of the local musicians felt affronted and patronised. Others, like the emerging Stiff

Little Fingers, felt that they could use the method in their own work. Encouraged by their management team, the SLF songbook became vivid with mention of incendiary devices, the behaviour of the Royal Ulster Constabulary and love across the barbed wire interzones.

Media outrage in the UK press about the Sex Pistols and the irreverence of their single 'God Save the Queen' gave loyalists an extra reason to dislike the local punks. When RUDI played at the Strathearn Hotel on 11 October 1977, a threat was received that the Holywood UDA were planning to arrive, heavy-handed. 'Thankfully,' says Brian Young, 'they didn't show up.'

RUDI had been inspired by a T. Rex concert on the Isle of Man in July 1975 and a generous encounter with singer Marc Bolan. Brian became a connoisseur of rock and roll – prepped on glam before discovering the New York Dolls and the fall-about cool of guitarist Johnny Thunders. He exchanged letters with other Thunders fans such as Steven Morrissey in Manchester. He got his guitar tuition by playing along to Chuck Berry records and, in time, RUDI managed a version of 'Pills' from the Dolls' repertoire. Later, they discovered it was a Bo Diddley original, but they told people in Belfast it was one of their own. Who would guess?

'We decided we'd just do our own thing,' Brian says. 'We'd been going to the Glenmachan Hotel at the weekends. It was notorious and underage – the most violent, horrible place – but we had nowhere else to go. We used to book private parties and then say, "Oh, there's a band playing". The band would be us. We played the Glenmachan and the Girton Lodge, which had a similar reputation. That was where we honed our chops. We would be playing maybe an hour and a half or two hours. It was a weird mixture – 60s garage, whatever Bowie and T. Rex we could figure out and a lot of old rock and roll songs.'

Brain razored and spiked his hair. Grimmy, the drummer, who worked with a clothes wholesaler, sidelined some nylon boiler suits. They hacked off the sleeves and wrote song titles and word-jams on the fabric with house paint: 'Pop Star' and 'New Commerciality'. Ronnie Mathews also sang and played guitar. In late 1977, Gordy Blair became the bass player after the band cut his hair and sourced extra-tall overalls, ready for the Trident on 17 November. They had a light show and an unassailable feeing that that were the best. Unlike those old hippies at the Pound...

'People came to see us and then once punk broke, people identified us. It sounds corny, but there was something in the air. You thought you were the only people who were into this stuff; you didn't realise that two streets away, there's two other people reading *Sounds* and *NME*. It was all working away. A lot of slightly younger people would have got into punk through reading the music papers and buying the first Ramones LP.'

Brian was apparently the first local to buy the Ramones album, on import from Caroline Music, a record shop that had been opened on Ann Street by Lawrence John in 1973. This was where Robin Brown and Kyle Leitch served up enthusiasm and knowledge, sourcing Tom Petty and Johnny Thunders imports, Sire pressings, whatever. For a time, Kyle was the de facto RUDI manager and an important connect. Other shops included Rocky Mungo's on

Steve Rapport

Linen Hall Street, Unicorn Records in Bangor and the four shops from the IT Records chain. Gigs by Dr Feelgood, Graham Parker and Eddie and the Hot Rods quickened the idea that music was getting sharper and more emotionally direct.

Brian made a visit to the shop soon after it opened and purchased a 'Back to Mono' badge, the discrete emblem of a Phil Spector fan. Young's meeting with Terri was an important connection across two dissenter traditions.

Early RUDI songs had been about drinking and youthful thrills, but 'Cops' was a response to the cancelled Clash concert at the Ulster Hall (20 October 1977) and the minor riot that ensued on Bedford Street. The chorus was a flat declaration: 'We hate the cops.' The verses conveyed some of the turbulence that had happened on Bedford Street and the black uniforms of the Royal Ulster Constabulary:

Standing at the Ulster Hall,

black bastards having a ball.

Punks are different, punks are strange,

but we ain't got no time to change.

Most remarkable of all was a chant that opened and closed the song. 'SS RUC' was a long-standing feature of football terraces, political protests and aerosol work on gable walls. It drew a comparison between the police force in Northern Ireland with the Schutzstaffel of Nazi Germany, entrusted by Heinrich Himmler to enforce security, terror and genocide. It was startling to hear this in a song and when RUDI played it live, their lighting guy, Marty Stitt, set off the sirens and flashing lights, recreating the anxiety and over-stimulation of a Belfast night.

RUDI played 'Cops' for the first time at Jordanstown Polytechnic on 13 December. When the bar staff heard it during the soundcheck, they told the band that on no account must it be performed during the gig. 'We played it as our last number anyways,' Brian says. 'No wonder they never asked us back!'

It was also in the set for the first punk night at the Pound on 12 January 1978. Terri was in the audience, driven there by Gordy's repeated demands. The punk-wary venue was tested by some new customers. Lights were smashed, the police came and returned with the Ulster Defence Regiment and so 'SS RUC' was played out by the band and seconded by the customers. It was the first local punk song about an actual event, naming the law enforcers and inciting the audience. Terri was thrilled. Mostly, he was taken by the generational change.

'I went down and I heard The Outcasts and I hated them with a passion. And I heard RUDI and I thought they were brilliant. And they did a cover of ? and the Mysterians' '96 Tears' because I was really big into American garage bands. Well, the police came in and started to check us all out. And then the kids all started shouting 'SS RUC'. And I remember one kid jumped up and pulled out a fluorescent tube light and threw it at them. I thought, "This is brilliant. This is what I've been waiting for all my life." I loved the anarchy of it. Then the UDR came in and they broke up the gig. So that, to me, was really exciting. We would have been a generation that were brought up to fear the police. That was the night I realised that the punks had no fear. I was really impressed by that.'

There are several origin stories about the beginning of Good Vibrations, the record label. This is Terri's version:

'I asked RUDI would they like to make a record, and my idea was to put out a flip-flop record (a flexidisc). And it cost 11p to put out a flip-flop record where you could actually put out a real record with EMI Dublin for 17p, so we went for the real record. And my intention was never to really run a record label. My intention was to put Northern Ireland back on the music map. Because even in the 60s, we had so much talent here. We had so many great people and great bands, but they all had to leave here to become successful. It was a chance for me to relive my youth.

'My ideas weren't always exactly what 16-year-old kids wanted. We didn't always see eye-to-eye about things. I must have seemed like an old man to them. But a lot of people just didn't get what I was at. I did think the whole punk movement was fairly subversive at the time but I also thought it was a great way of bringing young people together. Didn't matter

whether you're a Catholic or Protestant, didn't matter if your hair was orange or green, it mattered that you were a punk and I thought that was a brilliant thing. I wished I had have been that age and been a punk and been part of it. But I was an old hippie, and still am an old hippie – but I embraced the whole punk ethos.'

So, with another impetuous move, Good Vibrations Records was founded and RUDI had its first professional session booked for 7 February 1978. 'Big Time' was recorded at Templepatrick Studio, home to the Emerald Records stable of showbands, folk and parlour songs. The producer was George Docherty, who had also worked with the likes of Clubsound (and became a future co-conspirator of Jive Bunny). The backing tracks were recorded live and vocals were added afterwards in an assured rush.

It was magnificent. The sound of teen petulance and a truth attack on a posing scenester with a small soul who never bought the drinks. Brian's guitar was basic fare – an Antoria SG copy – but it went through an overloaded Carlsbro Stingray amp with the 'suzz' switch on full. His schooling in Chuck Berry and Johnny Thunders riffs was vividly reprised.

Ronnie Matthews delivered the vocal. The chorus was like a playground taunt, the voice of the young and the self-assured. On the flip side of the record, 'Number 1', Brian Young sang the lead. He declared that his picture should be on your sister's wall. RUDI were also about pop music. Marc Bolan had declared that you could sell lots of records and still be cool. The first release on Good Vibrations was a roaring statement, the sound of a generation looking beyond negativity, realising that the act of being successful was born in your head and in your heart.

A few weeks later, Terri picked up the delivery of the pressing in Dublin. He shared a ride with some friends, John Carson, Bernie McAnaney and Gerry Devlin.

'I remember it was torrential rain. The windscreen wipers weren't working. We eventually got to the EMI factory and I went in and they had the record pressed and they played it for us. And I just thought, "This is amazing". I couldn't believe that it had sounded so good. And it was just the excitement of having the seven-inch single and the wee girl in EMI asked could she have one and I went, "Of course – you can take a few".

'They gave give me a box and we went down to Dublin and I remember we couldn't find *Hot Press*. We eventually found it and we left one through the letterbox – a wee note and stuff. We actually managed to have a record out. And then we sent a copy to every record company in England that we could get an address for and most of them didn't even reply. It cost a fortune, but it was worth it.

'I started to feel that everything that I had done previously were all parts of the jigsaw puzzle. Like sending out a press release to say that we were having a demonstration. Like putting on folk gigs and stuff. Everything that I'd done before. And the record label was the final part. All of a sudden, the things that I'd learned from mistakes in the past seemed to just work for this moment in time. And it wasn't all easy. Not all the punks were all love and peace – far from it. But something really exciting was happening in Belfast. If I had of been a young person at that time, I would have thought this is just the most exciting thing ever. But I wasn't. I had my 30th birthday party in the Harp Bar one Christmas and I got up and I sang with RUDI and Protex. I had never thought I'd ever be up singing with a band. And that was great.'

An important thing had happened. Belfast was no longer just the subject of someone else's story. The punks in the North were telling it themselves.

Brian Young
Part 1

First time I encountered Terri Hooley was late summer 1977. I was 17 and spent most days, when I was supposed to be studying, wandering round Belfast city centre record shops with my pal, part-time delinquent and full-time truant 'Wee' Gordy Owen (aka 'Fangs Albert') from Sandy Row. I'd heard on the grapevine about a new record shop called Good Vibrations so we headed up to Great Victoria Street to investigate. Gotta say upfront that the name of the shop put me off as I never liked the Beach Boys – but a life-size figure of '56 era Elvis outside kinda allayed my fears.

After climbing the stairs to the first floor we musta been among the first customers as the shelves still smelt of fresh paint. First impressions were good – a long counter ran along one side of the room with the new stock and hundreds of 45s in the racks around the facing walls. A smaller back area contained second-hand albums. There were two older, hippy-ish guys behind the counter – a quieter (until you got to know him!) bearded guy called Dave Millar and another altogether more eclectic and animated beardster with a wonky eye who introduced himself as 'Terri with an i'.

We kinda hit it off pretty much from the get-go after I bought a Phil Spector 'Back to Mono' badge and we started yakking, discovering that we both shared a love of early 60s girl groups like The Shangri-Las and Ronettes (the Ronnie Spector photo on the wall was a dead giveaway and always given pride of place in Terri's shops down the years), 60s garage slop and 50s rock'n'roll/rockabilly. F'rinstance, we both adored the song 'Red Cadillac and a Black Moustache' by Warren Smith/Bob Luman, many years later recording a version of it for the *Big Time* EP Terri issued on local Belfast label Immortal Records.

Where the shop scored highest for me was the second-hand section, which was crammed with rarities and easily the best in Belfast. Amazingly, in hindsight, even though punk was pretty much mainstream by then, it didn't really seem to be on Terri's radar and in contrast to other Belfast shops like Caroline Music, Rocky Mungo's and Sounds Around, the shop stocked few punk platters. All that would change very soon – but none of those shops had anywhere near the huge variety of older stock that Good Vibrations specialised in – and the shop soon became a regular hang-out.

It's worth remembering that RUDI was the first punk combo in Belfast and we had been putting on our

RUDI at the Ulster Hall, 24 April 1980. Image by Geoff Harden.

own gigs throughout 1976/77 hiring function rooms in run-down dives like the Glenmachan [Hotel] and Girton Lodge in our native east Belfast. We rehearsed in a loyalist band hall off the Albertbridge Road and had even started writing our own songs. By Autumn 1977, as punk went overground, several other bands finally followed suit.

Eventually, Terri gave in to Wee Gordy's constant nagging and agreed to come down to see RUDI and The Outcasts play the Pound on 12 January 1978. The Pound was a notorious hippy hang-out and it was the first time they'd reluctantly let local punk bands set foot on their hallowed stage. Even though it was a weeknight, the place was packed and both bands alternated sets.

Terri hated The Outcasts but absolutely adored the racket we were making. Suitably enthused and energised, Terri started helping us where and when he could, arranging new practice rooms. I'm not entirely sure what the rest of the band made of Terri at first - at least one fellow band member was firmly convinced he swung (at the very least) both ways - but his enthusiasm was infectious and he was the first adult we'd ever encountered who actually seemed to take us seriously and for that we owe him a lot.

By now, too, Terri's pals Dave and Marilyn Hyndman who ran the Print Workshop on the floor above the record shop were already printing most of the local punk zines and posters for bands (I designed most all of the RUDI gig posters and Dave printed 'em real cheap) and 102 Great Victoria Street was rapidly becoming a vital meeting place and creative hub for the local punk scene.

The record label itself kinda happened by accident. *Alternative Ulster* zine, which was printed by the Print Workshop, wanted to give away a free RUDI flexi disc with the mag - like *Sniffin' Glue* did with ATV. As he was involved in 'the business', Terri offered to price this and when he discovered that it only cost a couple of pence more to do a proper vinyl record then we all decided to go for it! We played gigs to raise the money for studio/pressing costs and Kyle Leitch from Caroline Music, who was then our 'manager', organised studio time in Hyde Park Studios, Templepatrick, where we recorded 'Big Time'/'Number One' in a couple of hours on 7 February 1978. None of us had ever been in a studio before so we recorded both backing tracks live. George Doherty produced the record and did a really

great job. I only wish he'd produced our other Good Vibes records!

Terri then arranged for the actual pressing etc. We chose the sleeve design from artwork Terri's Art College buddies had put together. I think we picked the mummy artwork 'cos it had lipstick and we thought it was kinda New York Dollsy - totally unlike the clichéd punk sleeves that were common at the time. The sleeves were printed upstairs in the Print Workshop. 'Proper' sleeves were out of the question so when the records arrived back we had to sit and fold hundreds of A3 sheets - hey, it was the DIY ethic in action! Nobody really liked the folded sleeves much at the time as the paper wasn't hard-wearing and they were a pain to fold - but they became a Good Vibes trademark! We never signed any contracts - all profits were to be split 50/50 between us and the label. Thankfully, 'Big Time' sold really well and that enabled Terri to release more records. Locally, the impact was huge - if we could do it anyone could! It was that simple and a huge incentive to local acts - and pretty soon bands were clamouring for Terri to release their records.

With Terri's help we gigged constantly, headlining the 'Battle Of The Bands' at Queen's University in June 1978 - the first large-scale punk gig here featuring only local bands. The Harp Bar had become a regular punk venue and Victim and The Outcasts had recorded 45s for the label - but we reckoned we'd gotten as big as we could in Belfast and somewhat naively we decided to move to London in August 1978.

Terri was dead against the move - he'd seen all the Belfast bands he loved in the 60s follow a similar path with disastrous results but we were young, dumb and pig-headed and knew better!

Arriving in London, we soon realised we had gone from being big fish in a tiny pond to being minnows in a veritable ocean but we buckled down, ditched the boiler suits and rehearsed furiously, penning a whole new set of much improved material. We started picking up gigs too and were just starting to make waves when a run-in with the SPG landed Grimmy and Ronnie on remand in jail with the prospect of six months inside, each forcing us to return to Belfast. I have to say that while it was frustrating at times to see both The Undertones and SLF take off and media attention move, if only briefly, to Belfast while we were in London, I thoroughly enjoyed every minute of our time there. We had returned just in time to be filmed for *Shellshock Rock*, the John T. Davis documentary, which captured the nascent punk scene here at its peak.

In May, we recorded 'Laugh At Me' with Terri in a converted chicken shack studio in Ahoghill. In July, we travelled to Cork with Terri and The Outcasts for the premiere of *Shellshock Rock* at the Cork Film Festival. Surprisingly, the film was banned but, as a result, garnered great publicity in the media. Despite the ban it was shown on UCC's campus and followed by live sets from RUDI and The Outcasts. We also played with the film (and Terri) at the Belfast premiere in the Harp on 26 July, which was followed a couple of days later by the release of the *I-Spy* EP, at last.

'Laugh At Me' topped the indie charts in November, helped no doubt by the fact that Terri had ordered hundreds of copies of the record from Fresh, which compiled that week's Indie Chart. Funnier still, at the Harp Bar that Halloween, Terri had again joined us onstage for 'Laugh At Me' and was presented with a 'gold disc' for sales of the record! (It was a gold Lurkers flexidisc with a 'Laugh At Me' label glued on top!).

Despite the occasional one-upmanship and petty bickering it was still, at this point, very much a happy (if dysfunctional) family of sorts. Though we didn't perhaps realise it at the time, Terri really did want the best for his acts. Having a vibrant local label was hugely important – it provided the first real outlet for local talent, acting as a focal point for the local scene and attracting outside attention. At the same time, it gave us all a new and very tangible sense of pride in our own local identity. Mebbe for the first time here we were taking on the big boys and beating them at their own game. All real vital in a country where people were used to being treated as second-class citizens for far too long.

In the same way, the Harp encouraged people to start a band as now they had a ready venue to play in, Good Vibes provided a local vinyl outlet – so now anyone could make a 'proper' record of their own... after all, if we could do it then anyone could! The boost it gave to local confidence and the local scene in general can't be overestimated.

Ultimately, where Good Vibes fell down was that it never had any deliberate long-term strategy and was never run as a 'proper' record company. Nevertheless,

the success rate of the first run of Good Vibes 45s was pretty damn impressive, though latterly I fear that Terri began to believe his own hype, overlooking the fact that the bands themselves deserved at least equal credit for the success of the label – as it was they, not Terri, who had written and recorded the songs on which the label's reputation had been built. Meanwhile, he delighted in playing bands and band members off against each other – which was easy for him as he was over a decade older than any of us. F'rinstance, when Big Gordy was in the shop, he'd always play the Jilted John 45 so he could have the 'Gordon is a moron' refrain blasting out! Subtle or what? It's probably fair to say that most, if not all, of the bands/individuals on the label had an ongoing love/hate relationship with Terri at one time or another.

It's also fair to say that, perhaps understandably, the success of the label did go to his head and he began spending more time in the various local hostelries than behind the counter. To compound matters, the local distributors and wholesalers didn't like the competition and one in particular ran a constant dirty tricks campaign trying in vain to sabotage Good Vibrations' sales while trying to set up their own 'local' punk label to cash in on Good Vibes' success at the same time! Tellingly, they failed abysmally but it just shows ya what Terri was up against!

I was saddened to see the label fold as it left not only Belfast but the whole of Northern Ireland without a decent physical outlet for local bands. There were dozens of acts here in the 80/90s and beyond who would have thrived on the label and who deserved much wider exposure further afield but never got it. But them's the breaks...

Some folks still yammer on about what went wrong and for sure, Terri made a lot of mistakes and bad decisions, but there's no point now in moaning about what might have been and what could/should have happened. Terri was never a businessman (and never claimed to be) and he'd originally envisaged the label only as a stepping stone to help local bands get signed up and get the recognition they deserved – and it must be remembered that in that he largely succeeded.

At the Harp

Civic spaces in Belfast had been targeted from the start of the 70s and since Bloody Friday in 1972, the prime instrument had been the car bomb. As a result, the city centre was surrounded in 1974 by 17 steel gates, 10-12 feet high. Two years later and the plan was advanced to create a single security zone out of the four security quarters. This was 'the ring of steel'.

The social infrastructure was broken, as publican John McElhatton explains: 'In North Belfast there were 32 bars bombed out or burnt out in the early part of the Troubles. All these bars became waste ground or they became clubs – these social clubs that they all ran, in their own areas, where you had these bands mostly playing cover music. So, the original bands had no outlet. That was the problem. It was a result of the madness. In East Belfast it was something similar. There were a few bands like Baraka, with Rab McCullough, who had a major following in the West.'

Wes Graham and his cousin Colin 'Ziggy' Campbell had recently formed a band called Victim. The lack of a regular venue for new music in Belfast was a bother to them and so they walked through the city on a midweek afternoon in April 1978, looking for chances.

They tried a bar around Castle Lane, but since they were putting on strippers and doing fine, live music didn't interest them. The search moved on to Ann Street and again there was no success, but the musicians were advised to try a less obvious location, north of High Street, where Skipper Street became Hill Street. This was a dingy area that had once serviced the waterfront of the Farset River, a 17th century stopover for maritime workers and the poorest residential area in town. Later, it had been developed into stores and bonded warehouses for the distillers and blenders.

Journalists from the *News Letter* and the *Belfast Telegraph* drank at the Duke of York at Commercial Court and Gerry Adams served them pints. There were rebellious echoes back to the 18th century when Henry Joy McCracken and the United Irishmen had schemed around these alleyways and were hanged nearby. The Belfast Harp Festival of 1792 had convened a few hundred yards away at the old Assembly Room, when Edward Bunting had transcribed and preserved the airs of a dying breed. In 1978, the narrow, cobbled streets had not been

The Fall at the Harp Bar, September 1978. Image by Alastair Graham.

challenged by modernity. The area was badly lit and the bad reputation was warranted.

According to locals, the Harp Bar on Hill Street had once been called the White Horse. Customers came from the New Lodge and Divis areas. In mid-August 1975, a sub-machine gun was fired into the bar, injuring one person. On 30 August, around 8pm, a Ford Cortina pulled up and shots were fired at a bystander. One of the gang entered and threw in a bomb that killed a 30-year-old labourer, Denis McAuley, and fatally injured Sean Doherty, a docker and footballer who had played for Crusaders. The car was later abandoned at Dee Street and the UDA claimed responsibility, although it was suspected that other parties had also been involved.

Patsy Lennon, who ran a builders' yard on Hill Street, took over the Harp Bar, believing that it might provide a cash flow for the business. Early security measures involved six oil drums, filled with cement, ranged outside. By 1978 there was scaffolding and chicken wire and a security camera, allowing the bar staff to screen activity on the street. Other bars were using pre-constructed cages around the entrances, but the Harp stockade was adequate.

Importantly, it had a stage upstairs. One of Patsy's business initiatives had been to fly strippers in from Birmingham at the weekends. This was where they performed. Wes and Ziggy Campbell spoke to the bar manager, Maureen Cunningham, and asked her if they might put on a gig. She brought over the barman

Tony Douglas and she asked the two visitors what kind of music they played. Wes picked up on the conversation.

'We initially said we were a punk band but their jaws dropped so we swiftly changed tack to say that we were a new wave band, and that didn't really sit too badly with them. I guess they just didn't know what new wave was, so they said, "Yeah". It was an absolute dive but it had that all-important stage that we were chasing after and I remember it had one of those big glitter disco balls hanging from the roof and a little dance floor. So, it looked tacky but we both loved it.'

Victim played the Harp Bar on 21 April 1978, billed in the *Belfast Telegraph* as a 'New Wave Rock Group'. The support act was The Androids, featuring Joe Moody. As agreed, the bands took the door takings, and around 30 people turned up. Punk finally had a focal point in Belfast and, for teenagers like Maureen Lawrence, it was an immense reckoning:

'The Harp Bar, it was pretty much hardcore punks. That was the way it was meant to be: our club, our movement. The early days were great, especially when you had bands like The Outcasts and RUDI, The Androids, Stage B, Ruefrex... every one of those bands was different. The best nights you could possibly have. And if we went out, we all went together. We knew people came from all sides of the city and eventually they started coming from parts of the country. Nobody asked too many questions. The idea was, "You made it, you got here, we don't need to know any more than that".'

Joe Moody from The Androids had a gun pulled on him in the toilet of the Harp. He was wearing a soldier's beret: 'A para gave it to me in the early 70s

when I was a schoolboy. I thought it would be cool to wear it at gigs.' This wasn't a view that was shared by the regular drinkers downstairs, many of whom were republicans. It was rumoured that the Harp was frequented by 'Stickies' – the Official IRA. So, there were face-offs and some violent exchanges. When Ruefrex were performing the Sham 69 song 'Ulster', a gun was also pulled. But if the regulars downstairs were intimidating, then the punks upstairs could also have brutal tendencies. The daily aggression of Belfast life was reflected in the upstairs bar, even if it wasn't about religious sectarianism. Pretty Boy Floyd and The Gems (formerly the showband Candy) were roughed up and two members of The Tearjerkers were given hospital treatment and stitches after failing to impress the Harp regulars.

Terri and others were involved in the Punk Workshop. They contributed DJ equipment since the kit was often damaged or missing-in-action. Terri was their DJ for occasional reggae nights. Also, the Punk Workshop brought in acts from England. Its first import was The Fall, scheduled for 21 and 22 September, six months after the release of the group's first album, *Live at the Witch Trials*. A bootleg recording captured the raw connection between Mark E. Smith and Belfast, encoring with 'Industrial Estate' and 'Bingo-Master's Break-Out!'.

Other bookings included The Monochrome Set (24 and 25 November) and The Mekons (4 May 1979). London-Irish combo The Nipple Erectors came in for two shows (6 and 7 October 1978).

Terri knew the singer Shane MacGowan through his record-buying visits to the Rock On stall in Soho, London. Just ahead of the gig, Shane phoned Terri and asked if he should keep his head down. 'Just learn to keep your drink down,' Hooley advised. 'Words I now regret.'

There's a coda to the Mark E. Smith story in that The Fall were booked to perform at the Empire in Belfast, 8 November 1997. Smith had arrived at the gig in poor spirits. He kicked equipment around the stage and sacked the band.

In an attempt to try to calm the singer, staff at the venue rang Terri who later reported that Smith had been drinking champagne and was difficult to reason with. At one stage, Hooley grabbed the singer by the neck to restrain him. The singer thought he was about to get punched, and asked if he could remove his false teeth first. Hooley removed his own glass eye instead. 'I'm not gonna hit you,' Hooley insisted.

Smith then hit upon the idea of going onstage and playing an a cappella set of Beach Boys covers with Hooley and another friend. This option did not come to pass. Terri spoke to some disappointed fans at the venue when the news broke. 'Mark E. Smith is a dickhead,' he said.

I Need
Excitement

Terri made one of his best ever decisions while crossing the road at Bradbury Place. It was a defining call that left a beautiful mark on the history of popular music. He did not know the answer to the question when he started across the zebra crossing. But when he had reached the doors of Lavery's Gin Palace, he had his answer. Yes, he was going to put out a record by The Undertones.

He had not seen the band live and he knew little about their worth. There was no compelling reason to take a financial hit for the recording and pressing fees. It was a response to his friend Bernie McAnaney, a Derry guy who was enrolled at Queen's University. Bernie knew The Undertones from his hometown and he said they might break up if they didn't get a decent chance soon. Terri obliged.

He was following some strange law that he'd previously found on the lettering of his first ever record – the Humphrey Lyttelton flexi disc. You could count up the letters in your name and apply them to the words on the record label and it would

send back messages - like a hoodoo algorithm. Terri trusted the random energy of the universe and it led him to interesting places.

Also, he was never going to serve the profit motive. A decade of political thought had caused him to suppose that capitalism was the wrong steer. There were better reasons and he was not the only accidental entrepreneur. At the same time, when Terri was planning a fourth release on Good Vibrations (after records by RUDI, Victim and The Outcasts), a media figure in Manchester called Tony Wilson was formulating a local music project called Factory. His guiding method was praxis: 'You do something because you want to do it. And after you've done it, you find out all the reasons why you did it.'

For Hooley, the next challenge was to get the band into a recording studio in Belfast. There had been discussions in the shop about organising a benefit night for Dave Hyndman and his new idea, Just Books. The date for the gig was scheduled for 14 June 1978. So, The Undertones could play the fund-raiser and then record their tunes the following day. Terri

Terri and The Undertones at the McMordie Hall, 14 June 1978. Image by Patrick Simms.

RUDi
OUTCASTS
DETONATORS
UNDERTONES plus surprise bands
McMORDIE HALL Q.U.B.
Wed. 14th. June, 8 pm
Admission by ticket 80p from **JustBooks** 7 Winetavern Street
& **GOOD VIBRATIONS** 102 GT. VICTORIA ST.

needed a venue for his punk rock experience and he might need to apply some charm to secure it.

'So I went along to Queen's University. I got dressed up and, nice shirt and tie on, I went up to the Students' Union and I went to the office. And I said to this girl that we were the Belfast Music Society, and we wanted to put on a bit of a concert – some bands and stuff. I think that she thought that we were Queen's Classical Society. But she obviously wasn't the girl who did the normal bookings. She must have been on her lunch break, or something.

'She said, "Yes, Mr Hooley", and then she put it in the book and then she gave me a receipt. She asked me for five pounds, and I went, "Is that all you want?" And then when Queen's found out that it was seven punk bands, doing a benefit for the setting up of an anarchist bookshop, they weren't too pleased. And they tried to stop the gig. But we had a receipt and we were there. And then on the night of the gig, we got an awful lot of hassle from the bouncers. We had

the local bikers, the Chosen Few, they're doing security in front of the stage and one of the bands decided that they were never going to get a crowd as big as this and they wanted to play on, so we had to get the bouncers – the bikers – to put them off the stage gently.

'The Undertones came down from Derry to play. It was their first gig in Belfast. When they did the sound check they (the other bands) went, "Oh my god, we've got some competition here". And the gig went off very well. And because I'd been treated so badly, some of the kids decided they would put in some of the windows at the front of the Union. And a few days later, I got a letter telling me that I was banned for life from the Queen's Students' Union.

'So that was Belfast's first punk festival, really. We did some great gigs in the Ulster Hall, which the Belfast City Council wanted to ban. But I had bribed all the all the staff off – I gave them all a brown envelope with money in it and said to them if this concert goes

on, you get more money at the end the night. So when the city fathers phoned up and said, "We're a bit worried about this punk gig tonight", they said, "No, no, it'll be fine, it'll be grand, it'll be great".

'And I could never understand that the Belfast City Council wanted to ban our gigs when the IRA were blowing up the town and the murder gangs were out killing poor Catholics – and they wanted to stop us bringing kids together, just to pogo and have a good time. That was just ridiculous. I mean, if they thought punk was the threat, there was something wrong with them.'

In their formative days, The Undertones had bought their gear with credit vouchers from an instrument shop in Raphoe, Donegal. They learnt songs by The Rolling Stones, Cream and Fleetwood Mac and after they'd sourced records from a mate, Domhnall McDermott, they were up to speed with The Stooges, The New York Dolls and The Ramones. They finessed their set during an 18-month residency at the Casbah in Derry, a basic venue at the corner of Orchard Street and Bridge Street, set over a bomb site. The Casbah had no stage and punters were forbidden to pogo because it played havoc with the drinks shelves. If the young punks tried, Big Tony the barman would flick them with wet tea towels.

'It was a dinky and lovely place,' Feargal Sharkey recalls. 'It was basically a Portacabin. I believe it was dropped on top of the remains of the previous build. There was a lot of remodelling going on in Derry on a daily basis. It was an alternative to town planning. The outside of the Casbah had been covered in chicken wire and cement and was made to look vaguely Moroccan. There were two people at the first gig we played there (24 February 1977), but the barman let us back because he thought we were funny.'

Feargal was keen on Led Zeppelin and worked with Radio Rentals during the 1975 boom when Derry switched to colour television. He had the use of the company van and he made basic PA speakers out of which he could sing. The Undertones bickered plenty and by early 1978, they were on the verge of splitting and had to persuade their singer to stay for what they believed might be a legacy release. A series of English labels had already rejected their demo tracks and when John O'Neill heard the second Buzzcocks album, he felt that his band was after the event. They were not even sure about the merit of Feargal's tremulous voice, according to bassist Michael Bradley:

'It wasn't until people remarked on it that we realised that it was a very distinctive voice. But we used to have problems with him singing. I remember the early demos, and the singing was exactly what you would hear on the first LP, but Billy [Doherty, the drummer] said it was terrible. You basically went along thinking your band was awful.'

The studio budget was £200. Terri was outraged when they tried to charge him VAT. They had booked Wizard Studios, a modified clothing warehouse above Exchange Place. Four tracks, essentially recorded live, with an allocation for mixing a few days later. Davy Shannon set up the controls. Brothers John and Damien O'Neill constantly asked for their individual guitar levels to be raised until the fuzz quotient was perfectly overloaded.

They had worked through their Beatles records into girl-pop originals by The Shirelles and The Marvelettes, into soaring productions by Phil Spector with The Ronettes and The Crystals. Guitarist John O'Neill was a fan of the songwriting partners Jerry Leiber and Mike Stoller. Those tunes had been put to use by Elvis but it was their lyrics with The Coasters, like 'Charlie Brown' and 'Yakety Yak', that best

THE
UNDERTONES

TEENAGE
KICKS

captured the aches, scrapes and frustrations of youth. The guitarist also loved the soundtrack to *American Graffiti*, released in 1973. All this had a bearing on 'Teenage Kicks'. The titled hinted at 'Route 66'. Likewise, 'Teenage Lust' by MC5. And then Feargal took the heartbreak to another, overwhelming level.

'We had already made cassette recordings in Mrs Simm's shed,' he says, 'and then we'd made a demo on a four-track studio at Magee University in Derry. So, when we got to Wizard Studios, we weren't particularly overawed about what we had to do in four hours. By the time we did that session, we were pretty good.'

Terri was of the same opinion. 'The Undertones were fantastic because they practised a lot. And they practised and practised and practised, and that's what every band should do. And they could have just recorded it live, basically. They were brilliant and I didn't like studios – I thought it was a waste of time because I'm not a musician. And I know nothing about music. I remember going down with some sandwiches and crisps and lemonade and stuff for the band and I heard 'Teenage Kicks' and I just thought it was the greatest thing ever.'

The release date was 31 August. As with previous Good Vibrations releases, the sleeve was an A3 design printed by Dave Hyndman and folded, origami-style, to house the record, which had the heft and delicacy of a dinner plate. Hooley had taken a box of records to London but the industry was not impressed. He got a few copies into John Peel's pigeonhole at Broadcasting House while the band worked their own connections to the DJ. Yet Terri's trip seemed rather pointless.

'I went to Rough Trade, who were the biggest independent distributors in England at the time. And they'd just signed up Stiff Little Fingers and I was sure they were going to sign up The Undertones and they told me it was the worst record they ever heard in their life. And I was broken-hearted and I nearly cried. I took it to EMI and CBS and everybody else that I could get a meeting with and they all told me the same thing.

'Then I came home on the Monday and broke down and cried to my wife and said, "These people in England have no idea what real music's all about. And they pay more for designing a record sleeve than what it actually cost us to record 'Teenage Kicks'." She said, "Well, maybe John Peel will play it". And John played it that night (9 September) and then he played it twice (25 September) – that was the first

time in the history of the BBC that a record had been played back-to-back.'

The Radio 1 DJ Peter Powell made it his record of the week and when Peel heard it played during that slot, he pulled the car to the side of the road, weeping uncontrollably. Seymour Stein, boss of Sire Records, caught the record on the Peel show and dispatched his charge, Paul McNally, to Derry to sort out a deal. Terri Hooley was out of his depth and largely uninterested in the finances. Eventually, he settled for £1,000, nominally for two of the four EP tracks: 'Teenage Kicks' and 'True Confessions'.

Meantime, Feargal and Mickey tried to negotiate a deal for the band in London, claiming that Derry's finest were on a par with The Clash and The Rich Kids. They walked away with a worse deal than The Bay City Rollers but they were on *Top of the Pops* within weeks and John O'Neill had plenty to offer yet. Again, there was appreciation for Terri. This time it was John who put a value on his contribution:

'He was like Neal Cassady, without the amphetamines – he had the energy of a speeding train about to go off the rails and, at first, I found it quite overwhelming. However, when we discussed music, you'd tell straight away he knew what he was talking about and how much passion he felt about it.'

It was not a wealth-making transaction. Once again, Hooley had revealed his anti-Midas tendencies.

'Well, I've always said the worst thing that could ever happen to an independent record label was to have a hit single. Anybody else in the music business would have gone on to sign a contract with The Undertones and to license the record to them. I would have made money, but it wasn't what I was all about, because I'd grown up in poverty. Not real, bad poverty, but poverty enough. The money was not my goal. I seen what money had done to people when they'd won the pools and stuff, and it just didn't interest me. I was more interested in putting Belfast on the music map. So I missed my big opportunity to be rich there.'

Michael Bradley admires his conduct with the band:

'The great thing about Terri was that he had no intention of saying, "I have a valuable property here". Anyone who knows Terri will know that making money is not at the heart of what he does. So, he really just introduced the record company guy to us. We then signed a record deal with Sire. Terri was there at the first meeting. Then Terri says, "Bye bye".'

I'm Just
an Outcast

reg, Martin and Colin Cowan became The Outcasts in 1977 after being refused entry to a series of bars and clubs. Unlike the Ramones, they actually were brothers. Guitarist Colin 'Getty' Getgood was their long-standing guitarist and they had travelled to see Alice Cooper in Liverpool and Bowie at Wembley. They had a bristling, bad-boy dynamic, living at speed, adopting the manner of Brando in *The Wild One* and released their debut single 'Frustration' in spring 1978. This was on the IT label, a Portadown-based enterprise that had previously released 'Big City' by Speed and 'Punk-Rockin' Granny' by The Duggie Briggs Band. The Outcasts had a firm presence at the Harp, and on one occasion they returned a PA system to Harry Baird's rental shop with human teeth embedded in the speaker cabinet. The pattern of uproar had been established at their very first gig in August 1977, at Paddy Lambe's bar in Ballyhackamore, east Belfast.

'At the end of that first gig,' Greg remembers, 'the guy walked into the dressing room and said, "Who's playing the national anthem?" And Getty, God love him, reckoned he could struggle his way through it. He went out and he got pelted, absolutely pelted, with coins and everything. 'Cos they thought he was doing it to take the piss out of them. It was horrific. We had this mentality of us against the world. And the violence – I like to joke now that it was cartoon violence – it was not fucking cartoon-like when you were getting beat up by us. If something did kick off, The Outcasts made it worse.'

Terri had been unimpressed by the band when he watched them play with RUDI at the Pound in 1978. But the admiration followed and Good Vibrations released their next single, 'Justa Nother Teenage Rebel', in 1978 and the label's first album, *Self Conscious Over You*, in 1979.

The Outcasts name-checked the Harp Bar in a later song called 'Gangland Warfare':

'The words tell a story. The Harp was like a little haven but to get to and from it was a nightmare. We used to do a walk to and from the Harp when the Midlands opened and you walked along York Street and that was like something out of *The Warriors* film.

SELF CONSCIOUS OVER YOU
THE OUTCASTS

Terri and Getty from The Outcasts, Downtown Radio, 1983. Image by Alastair Graham.

There really were gangs that were waiting for you coming - to prey on kids. The guys who went to the Harp were real, they were from Rathcoole, from the Antrim Road, they fought their way down, fought to be punks in their own areas. You didn't fuck with those guys.'

The Outcasts were happy to play outside Belfast, where the audience might not be appreciative. In April 1979, they were part of a Good Vibrations package tour with RUDI and The Tearjerkers, playing the likes of Ballymena, Cookstown and Omagh.

'It was Terri's idea to play around Northern Ireland. You would turn up even somewhere like Dungannon, and there was no nightlife. Police stations looked like military encampments. Cinemas were all bombed. You've no idea how bad those towns were and we'd turn up and play a showband hall that maybe held 400 people with a 100-watt PA and a 35-minute set, and the whole town would come. There were always wee guys with badges and big coats standing at the side of the stage. It did work for us. That's how we got our following. We played anywhere that would have us. We played in the middle of the Creggan in Derry, we played Crossmaglen, we played Strabane. I think we genuinely helped towards the political situation in Northern Ireland without being political. I think we did go some way between breaking down that barrier of only mixing from your own area. That's my proudest legacy.'

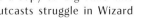

Terri also recalls the transformational power of punk rock on tour. 'The first night was in Glenarm and it pissed out of the heavens we thought nobody'd be there. Davy Miller was driving me down past Larne and we saw this poor girl with a rucksack in the rain and I said, "Well, we better stop and give her a lift". And I said, "Where are you going?" She says, "Glenarm". I said, "Why are you going to Glenarm? Nobody goes to Glenarm." She says, "Oh, all these fantastic bands have come over from Scotland" – it blew our minds. We were going, "What are these bands called? Never heard of them." And then we said, "We'll go in with you to make sure you're okay" and then we went in and introduced her to the bands and I said, "There you are", and looked after her that night.

'And on the way out, the guy in the bar had enough and they wouldn't let anybody back into the bar. I was dying to do a piss and I saw this wall, and everyone said, "No, no, no". I didn't see the river between and I fell into the river. We were coming out and the UDR were stopping everybody and I was sitting in the front, bollock-naked. And they sent this UDR woman over to ask me had I any identification on me and they're going, "He's coming from that bloody punk gig down there!" So that was interesting.

'We took punk where no punk had gone before. I remember there was a bar in Armagh and everybody was dressed like Rory Gallagher. They didn't much like the bands and then I got up and did 'Laugh at Me' – with a duck hat on my head off a Neil Innes album. They really liked that.'

Film director John T. Davis took his early inspiration from the sight of D.A. Pennebaker in 1966, hoisting a camera on his shoulder, walking backwards out of the Grand Central Hotel on Belfast's Royal Avenue. The American was shooting Bob Dylan for his *Eat the Document* tour film and this combination of music, art and frayed circumstance had a great bearing on John's own method. Based in Holywood, County Down, he would also use hand-held cameras and wait for the rough illuminations. He applied this ethos on *Shellshock Rock*, a piercing documentary of the Northern Ireland punk scene.

He managed on a budget of £7,500, aided by a great deal of professional favours. He worked over the winter of 1978-79, showing a city in the doldrums, soundtracked by a Salvation Army band and the rolling tonnage of military armour. The poor light accentuated the grain and the feeble wash of Christmas illuminations. It was important to put in the setting because the music and the liberated faces of the music fans were so alert.

He shot The Undertones, declaring 'Here Comes the Summer' in the pure dinge of the Pound. There was footage of Stiff Little Fingers and 'Alternative Ulster' at the University of Ulster - a moment that was almost missed until Derek the soundman fixed a plug with a soldering iron just 30 seconds before showtime. John edited comedic music into the narrative from James Young and when he followed RUDI to a storm-lashed Orange Hall in the Craigantlet Hills, he inserted 'Rhythm of the Rain' by The Cascades, sweetly love-sick in California.

The potential of punk constantly lights up the participants. Terri holds up a copy of 'Big Time' like a miraculous relic. The Outcasts struggle in Wizard

Studios, a mess of swearing, rough musicianship and inarticulacy. Eventually, they win. Protex sing into the distorted night of 'Strange Obsessions' and The Idiots make playful havoc out the Dion fave 'A Teenager in Love'.

There's a scene at a youth club in Andersonstown where a kinder-punk band called The Parasites are doing their own song called 'Society'. They lack the cool references of the older acts around town. The music is a received clatter of two chords and rote phrases. Yet, they too are open to a provocative strain of thought that is reaching out from discerning record collections into housing estates and Third Form dinner breaks. Elsewhere in the film, 18-year-old Eugene Goldsmith rides through the city in the back of John's black Simca station wagon and articulates a descending truth:

'It's things like this that are gonna spark it off, y'know. Everything's gonna change sooner or later. It happens in small forms like music and crap like that. It starts changing, slowly, but it'll all change eventually. When people will kick in the whole way to live and just start from scratch again.'

Terri had his own encounters with young music fans who might have gone in another direction. He remembers a teenager called Joe, who had tried to steal an Outcasts album from the shop:

'And I said, "How much money have you?" And he said, "I got 50 pence". I said, "Give me the 50 pence, there's the album". Later, Joe said to me one night in Voodoo, "Well, in those days, I had two choices: one,

I decide to be a punk, or [two] I join the IRA. And I decided, "Fuck the Provos – I'm gonna be a punk." So maybe it did help save people's lives. I'm not sure, but I think it changed a lot of people's lives.'

'A Sense of Ireland' was a six-week cultural programme in London, starting 3 February 1980. There were over 90 events in 44 venues, involing Seamus Heaney, The Chieftains, the Abbey Theatre plus Rory Gallagher at the Venue on St Patrick's night. Directed by John Stephenson, the aim was to present a confident and evolving review of the island. There were political and artistic representations of the North at the Action Space on Chenies Street. Good Vibrations was invited to put on a showcase at the Venue on Victoria Street, 16 March. Terri brought over RUDI, The Tearjerkers and The Moondogs. It was a positive story but not everyone was pleased, as he recalls:

'I had been told that my bands shouldn't play this festival because it didn't represent what was happening in Northern Ireland – the strip searches in Armagh, the boys in the Kesh and things like that. And I said, "We're going. You can shoot me, but don't shoot the bands." At the press conference in London, a woman said, "We have Terri Hooley, who has been threatened, but has decided to bring the bands over". I thought, "Thank God it's late in the afternoon and the *Belfast Telegraph* has gone to press and nobody's gonna pick this up". I didn't want this blasted over the newspapers. I was certainly afraid of these people but there were many times I stood up to them. I'm a natural born coward, but I did it. I used to get threatened all the time. Very serious threats from some quarters. And years later, I got apologies.'

Fire-damaged artwork by John T. Davis for *Self Conscious Over You*.

SELF CONSCIOUS OVER YOU

John T. Davis made a short film about the Outcasts, *Self Conscious Over You*. It was filmed at the Ulster Hall on 24 April 1980. John Peel had flown over to play tunes and introduce the music, which was significant. Ruefrex were making the case for a more literate direction on the Good Vibrations roster. Big Self were adventurous and abstract, searching for new tones, not wanting to be limited by the expectations of the scene. Shock Treatment stepped into a vacant slot and acquitted themselves well. RUDI suffered from equipment issues as the stage became busy and the Ulster Hall stage filled with unruly fans. The Outcasts were going through their skinhead phase, ramping up the aggression and the audience cheered at the spectacle.

This was probably the high point of Good Vibrations. The shop was hosting this bold event alongside Session Music, a music equipment firm. Terri's label was now perceived as an off-ramp to a bigger record deal. It had worked for The Undertones, Protex, The Tearjerkers, Victim and Xdreamysts. The success of RUDI seemed like a given. Yet media attention had shifted to Manchester, Glasgow, Leeds, even Dublin, where bands were taking up a post-punk challenge, making wiry noise and inventing the new. Good Vibes had diversified with non-Irish releases and was set to press up the reggae experiments of Dublin's Zebra on 12-inch vinyl.

But it was a coming age of irony, the postmodern and expensive, cantilevered pop. Good Vibrations routinely told the press that it was financially busted. But forever obstinate, as Terri told the *NME*: 'I'm not making records for the English record market. I'm making them for the local market. We've had offers of partnerships – phoenix rising from the ashes type shit – but I just couldn't work with people who are involved with money all the time.'

Hooley's other response was to release his own single on Fresh Records, a version of the Sonny Bono hit 'Laugh at Me'. It was ludicrous, as he had intended. 'The single was good fun. At least I did it. The whole thing was done as a joke. It gave me a chance to get onstage. I want to say to people, "If I can do it, there's nothing to stop you doing it as well".'

Terri sang 'Laugh at Me' on the stage of the Ulster Hall, after The Outcasts' set. He was mobbed by kids, who chanted 'Terri is our leader'. He sang tunelessly, with gusto. He invited the laughter and he wore the delirium like a stage outfit. It was magnificent. It was pure folly.

1980

The Ulster Hall, 24 April 1980. Terri, John Peel, The Outcasts and Shock Treatment. By Geoff Harden.

Listening
to Marvin

Bill Kirk

GOOD VIBES APPEAL

WE HAVE WON THE CASE TO REOPEN,
BUT....
THE COURTS REQUIRE THAT WE RAISE £2000 TO INJECT INTO THE BUSINESS BEFORE THEY WILL GIVE US BACK THE KEYS OF THE SHOP.
WE WOULD LIKE 20 PEOPLE TO LEND US £100 EACH.

I NEED YOUR HELP!

CONTACT — TERRI HOOLEY,
4 WOLSELEY ST,
BELFAST 7.
Ph. 248651.

Terri was playing tunes in Holywood when some radio people came to see him. He was at a venue called The Deep but everybody called it The Dive. He was up by the old cinema projection booth, doing a DJ favour for a friend. He went down to see the visitors but someone kicked some dust around and Terri got a fleck of metal in his good eye. He went to a specialist to get it looked at.

'The guy said to me, "How long have you known you were going blind?" I said, "First I ever heard of it". They said they weren't sure. Then about a year later, they told me I wasn't. All I did that year was play Marvin Gaye's *What's Going On*. I think it just went along with my worry – worrying about the fuckin' world, and life.'

Good Vibrations went bankrupt in April 1983. Terri's tax reporting had been erratic and his debts were

£20,000. He argued that his assets were worth that amount and his accountant, Brendan N. Lynn, set out a case for an appeal. There were extenuating circumstances, such as the separation from his wife, a period of worsening problems with his eyesight and vinyl stock that had been unaccounted for during his time away from the business.

The Good Vibrations record label, stated Brendan, was an 'unprofitable diversification' and that contracts with successful acts were not binding due to his client's 'soft-hearted approach'. Finally, there was one creditor who had a long-standing and significant account with Terri, who might have enjoyed a future business relationship if the relatively small debt was somehow managed and extended.

Was there a concerted push to take Terri out of business, hence, the demand for immediate payment? Certainly, Terri's success had upset some of the old-school music figures in the North. A few companies

had even contrived their own 'punk' products, designed to meet this new market. They dressed their records in brown paper bags and feigned the street-cred manners that were second nature to Good Vibrations. There was a jealous backstory and Terri believed that his rivals were even scheming together as a cartel to remove him from the business.

Terri's friends in the local press wrote sympathetic stories and he obliged them with a photo session at the local social security office. Jim Cusack, a friend from the *Irish Times*, delivered a strong testimonial for the cause: 'A feeling of nausea comes over me as I think of the ugly faces of others who have made packets out of the music business in Northern Ireland and not given a ha-pence worth back to the boys and girls who made them rich. Would that there was a Robin Hood-type character who could rob these rich shitheads and give to the poor, starving Good Vibes people.'

Unfortunately, the debt was a deal-breaker and the company folded. Terri had anticipated his demise in an interview with *Melody Maker* in 1979: 'We'd rather be failures than be owned.'

Carrie Davenport

Bradley Quinn

Terri with Michael
Callaghan (left)
and Hearts of Steel

Ghoul's Out

There was financial ruin in the air, but in 1982, Terri also wore the fright wig and was on manoeuvres with The Legendary Rocking Humdingers. This was his latest pick-up band – associates from the jazz scene and the act Apartment. They had recorded 'Dracula's Daughter', a fave from the repertoire of Screaming Lord Sutch in 1962. The flip side was 'The Hokey Cokey' and on both tracks, the vocals were essentially tuneless and rhythmically challenged. It was classic Terri. He sometimes arrived onstage in a coffin.

'We don't care what people think,' Terri told a *Hot Press* writer. 'If they think we're fools, it doesn't matter, we're not gonna leave them without making them laugh – at us or with us, it doesn't matter.'

Owing to the bankruptcy proceedings, the record may not have been officially released. But it escaped like a strange odour and music fans were perplexed at the typo on the record sleeve. The 'n' was missing, so the combo was merely the Humdigers. Also, the graphics were so messy that some collectors supposed that the band was The Legendary Rocking Bumdigers. They were the butt of many jokes.

Some of Terri's other outfits fared better. The Hearts of Steel had various conscripts but Jimmy Symington was a regular guitarist and was sympathetic to the loose working method. Jonny Quinn, a sometime shop assistant in Good Vibes, played drums. He later joined Snow Patrol and enjoyed

better terms and conditions. This line-up was completed by Nick 'Loopy' Hamilton. Allegedly, Terri broke up the band because they were getting too professional.

There were sporadic dates around Terri's release of the RUDI song 'Big Time' in 1999. Brian Young played guitar and Paul Rowan banged a gong. In more recent years, Terri's onstage consigliere has been the guitarist Michael Callaghan. Quality control has varied, but there have been remarkable, spontaneous moments with the Ben Harper song 'Excuse Me Mr.'. Also, Terri has been known to transform the Tim Rose murder ballad 'Hey Joe' into an exorcism of the Irish conflict. 'UVF, IRA, how many men did you kill today?' he would chant, and sorry tears would roll.

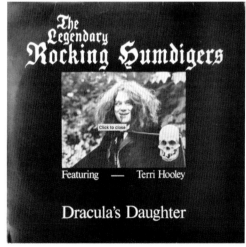

Rock
Around
the Shops

Closing night at Howard Street

Winetavern Street

After the bankruptcy of 1983, Terri returned with a series of guises and locations, firstly across the road from the old shop at 121 Great Victoria Street. The premises was bomb-damaged in 1992. He moved to 54 Howard Street, where the footfall was good and visitors included Britt Ekland, The Beastie Boys and Van Morrison. The paramilitary ceasefires of 1994 led to an upswing in tourism, but just as business became viable, so the multinational record shops were given sweetheart deals to set up in the city and displace the local indies.

Thereafter, Terri circled the more affordable fringes of the city. The arson attack on the North Street Arcade (see overleaf) was a shocking, unresolved crime. Terri kept the faith at Phoenix Records, Haymarket Arcade before a more settled stay on Winetavern Street. His final location was above the Bigg Life project on 93 North Street, which he vacated in June 2015 after various health issues.

Good Vibrations really was a way of life. On Boxing Day 2010, Terri invited friends to visit the Winetavern Street shop for a party. The guests were asked to bring down a photograph of someone they had recently lost. Those pictures were placed on the wall. Terri always said that a favourite record was 'It's Gonna Be a Cold Cold Christmas' by Dana. So, with beautiful intuition, he took these souls away from the commercial overkill in the city centre, giving them a place to grieve and relate.

Bill Guiney at Howard Street

Rosie McMichael at Howard St

The rebranded Sounds Around shop   Winetavern Street   With Alex at Winetavern Street

Frankie Quinn

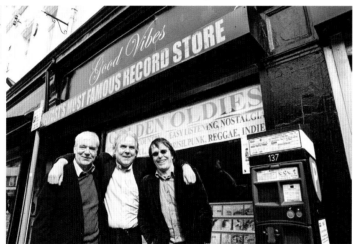

Winetavern Street with Willie Richardson and Ciaran McWilliams   Phoenix Records at Haymarket Arcade

Howard Street   The last shop on North Street

They Burnt Us Out

2004

Terri was at a Maritime reunion gig at the Empire Music Hall on 17 April 2004. It was a celebration of the R&B scene that had energised Belfast 40 years before. Hooley was set to introduce Billy Harrison, original guitarist with Them, when his friend, Biggy Bigmore phoned up.

'North Street Arcade is on fire,' he said.

'What part of it?'

'All of it.'

Terri was firstly worried that some of his fellow shopkeepers and creative friends might have been caught in the blaze. His friend Leslie used to nap in his studio above his shop. Anita, the owner of arts boutique The World Turned Upside Down, would sometimes work through the night. To his relief, Terri noticed that both of them were at the gig. But at least 20 businesses had been incinerated, including the Arcadia Café, the Factotum arts project, Bill Burlingham's bookshop, the office of the Cathedral Quarter Arts Festival and Biggie's rehearsal rooms. All of the animals in the pet shop were burnt alive. Terri lost his records, Good Vibrations artwork, letters and master tapes. There was irreplicable stuff like a signed Johnny Cash photo and his picture of Ronnie Spector.

A forensic report revealed that there had been a series of fires at both entrances to the Art Deco, listed building. An experienced arsonist had placed devices at the North Street and the Donegall Street entrances. Terri believes that someone was hired in from England and had been spotted the day before, scoping out the plan of the place.

'We practically lost the history of the label, 'cos I moved a lot of stuff out of my house. Good Vibrations was never the same after North Street Arcade. It was all fucking downhill after that. But it was just pride. I had to have a record shop.'

No prosecutions for the arson attack have been forthcoming.

The Hooley Gang

A gang of errant musicians and pals gathered for a press call on Gordon Street, Belfast on 13 March 2008. It was a chill afternoon and they looked like extras from a Peckinpah film, but the mission was a decent one. Terri's friend Arthur McGee had planned an event called 'Good Vibrations - A Light in the Darkness'. It was a fund-raiser for the shop, featuring The Undertones, Shame Academy, Panama Kings and special guests. Gary Lightbody came down for the launch and so did writer Glenn Patterson and film-maker John T. Davis.

The gig took place at the Mandela Hall on 25 April. On the night, James Nesbitt read out a statement from former US President Bill Clinton.

'By supporting young musicians in Northern Ireland and introducing them to audiences in England and elsewhere, Good Vibrations not only helped individual musicians to realise their dreams but also offered listeners the opportunity to better understand and appreciate one another through the common language of music.

'While I'm proud of my contribution in bringing about the Agreement, I know that no government policy can truly succeed without grass-roots efforts of those people the policy would effect. I commend Terri Hooley and all those involved in Good Vibrations, for giving young people something positive to say yes to.'

Fly Away Peter

Terri and Alex were packing away stock at the Winetavern Street shop on 16 September 2011. The artist Anne McCloy rang. She was on her way over in a taxi with Pete Doherty, the former Libertine. He arrived and checked out a Shangri-Las record on the racks. Moments later, he was singing 'Teenage Kicks' and Terri had uncorked a bottle of red wine.

They visited Biggy Bigmore at his arts studio on North Street before heading over to the Oh Yeah Music Centre, where Pete admired the Strummerville rehearsal rooms and told unrepeatable stories about Amy Winehouse in Berlin. Later, there was a visit to the Ulster Hall, where the Good Vibrations film crew was recreating the 1980 show when Hooley sang 'Laugh at Me' for an encore. The real Terri eyeballed Richard Dormer, who was playing himself. There was an actor on the far side of the stage, dressed as Hank Williams, part of a dream sequence.

At some point Terri left for the Mandela Hall, where he introduced Pete onstage. He was exiting the venue at the back when he tripped on a concrete wall and hurt his foot. He got a lift home and fell through the door. Claire figured he had probably just sprained his ankle. 'She put me in the recovery position, threw a blanket round me and went to bed.'

The following Friday, Terri took part in a parade as the elected Lord Mayor of the Cathedral Quarter. He was walking with the help of a stick. On the Monday he visited the doctor. 'The doctor says, "You've a broken leg, how did you stick the pain for ten days?" I says, "Well, the drink and the drugs certainly helped".'

He travelled to Dundalk for a documentary interview and a wrap party for the film. There was no moderation, no sleep 'til Belfast. 'There's a photograph of Greg pushing me in the wheelchair out of the hotel the next day with a can of Harp in my hand.'

Terri is
our Leader

It is August 2011 and *Good Vibrations*, the film, is a real concern. The production team is casting for parts. Indie kids are being chosen to play punk faces from 1978. Veterans are taking roles as paramilitaries, dockers, community activists and even the old guys who drank downstairs at the Harp Bar, hating the rock and roll teenagers who had invaded their patch. It's an amusing time.

A facsimile of the old record shop has opened on North Street, a lovely visitation. Elsewhere, Anna Carr, Terri's daughter, is playing a nurse during the recreation of her own birth. Her father is spending time with Richard Dormer, who will assume the role of himself. The actor had previously morphed into Alex Higgins, snooker savant and elemental force in his own stage play, *Hurricane*. Now he is going through a Hooley transference. The 70s beard is emerging and the mannerisms are starting to flex.

Richard first visited Terri at his shop on Winetavern Street and they had breakfast nearby in Smithfield market. But the real understanding began at the John Hewitt, when the drinks were in and Hooley was throwing his arms about, embracing the world. '*That's* Terri now,' his mates said. Then, when he watched *Shellshock Rock*, Richard noticed how the guy talked about RUDI and 'Big Time' and used the word 'fantastic' with such relish. There was rhythm and wonder in his style. Another important learning moment arrived when Richard was fitted with a lens on his left eye. He decided not to have a pinhole in the prosthetic. Then he turned the lens around to

create an ill-fitting, Health Service utility look. He began walking with his shoulder out, bracing his blind side for obstacles and unwanted encounters. He was walking the talk.

Terri's perennial chat-up line has been to anoint each new female companion as 'the future Mrs Hooley'. But the production team of the *Good Vibrations* story gave this routine an amusing spin, calling Richard 'the future Terri Hooley'. All this was magnificently assumed during a night at Horatio Todd's pub in east Belfast. Dormer was communing with Hooley, trying out his array of tics, cackles and roars. At the end of the night, he ordered himself a taxi in the persona of his new character. The actual punk supremo watched his doppelganger at work. At the end of the phone call, the taxi firm asked whom the car was calling for.

'Terri,' said Dormer, without cracking a smile. 'Terri Hooley.'

The film project had started more than ten years earlier. Terri had encountered the writer Glenn Patterson and some Dublin media figures in the Crown Bar. He had given them his life story in the snug – all the true accounts and the embroidered

extras. Glenn reckoned there was a tremendous narrative in all this. There were further meetings and the writer Colin Carberry came on board. A treatment was delivered and the media people were intrigued. But Terri wouldn't sign away his rights. He wasn't feeling it.

By 2007, there were parallel interests. The writers had spoken to film-makers Glenn Leyburn and Lisa Barros D'Sa, who were at work on their debut, *Cherry Bomb*. The composer David Holmes was part of their production company, Canderblinks. Around the same time, Gary Lightbody and Snow Patrol were getting enthused and wanting to help with brokering some finance. So was Andrew Eaton, who became the project's Executive Producer. All this started to converge.

The idea was considered by BBC Films before reaching Film Four, who helped with development but ultimately wanted the storyline

Jodie Whittaker and Richard Dormer

to stress the conflict and how the young punks were impacted. Terri was nervous about his own portrayal, that they wanted him to be a bomb-strafed Richard Branson. The project faltered. There had been help from the UK Film Council, which had supported a short pilot in 2010 – the first appearance of Richard Dormer as a potential Terri. The team had dressed up the basement of the Menagerie Bar and restaged the 1978 moment when Terri first saw RUDI and the Outcasts at The Pound. Even in this scratchy production, there was kinetic energy, intelligence and soul.

David Cameron became the British PM in 2010 and brought in his austerity policies. The UK Film Council was stripped out and the industry was waylaid. Yet, in time, *Good Vibrations* was back with BBC Films and rolling again. The growing gang of instigators also included a Parisian record pimp and graffiti artist plus Bruno Charlesworth, an Australian arts entrepreneur, the Irish producer Chris Martin, the Irish Film Board and NI Screen.

The casting for *Good Vibrations* was visionary. Jodie Whittaker and Richard Dormer and Adrian Dunbar became high profile figures afterwards, but they did not stint on the Belfast work. Dylan Moran was an embattled publican and Ryan McParland was a breathless rendition of Gordy Owen, demanding Buzzcocks records and insisting that Hooley should come and see amazing punk bands at The Pound. Even Terri got his cameo part as a hapless folk artist with a Clancy Brothers cap and báinín jumper. He was clogging up studio time when The Undertones were primed for glory. 'I should have won an Oscar,' he mused later. 'Best Accordion Playing in a Movie.'

Unlike many Belfast films, it didn't use the conflict as a lazy device. It was confident in its own worth, untouched by cultural cringe. The one-liners were memorable and caustic, a homage to Belfast and its terse manners. It was sentimental, but not soft. At the early screenings when the house lights went up, many in the audience were tearful.

Maureen Lawrence was an original punk and the experience was important to her. She had campaigned for a plaque at the site of the old Harp Bar location

on Hill Street, which was unveiled by Terri in 2012. He had walked his people to the spot, calling his punk parade 'our traditional route' and he rubbished the Lord Mayor in an entertaining, scattershot ramble.

Next, there was a feature film for Maureen to contend with, loaded with memories and values for her generation.

'We all ended up getting married and having children,' she says. 'We call them the 'lost years' before everybody re-grouped later on. When I first watched *Good Vibrations* at the Ulster Hall it was emotional, and we were having a great laugh about it and just delighted that somebody had done this film and the soundtrack was great. But when I went to see it the second time and took my kids and sat in the middle of them, I cried all the way through it. Because when we watched the premiere, it was Terri's film and his life story. But when it watched it the second time it was as much my story as anyone else's. Every time the

Good Vibrations preview screening at the QFT, May 2012. Image by Stuart Bailie.

Terri and David Holmes Image by Stuart Bailie.

bombs went off, my kids kept looking at me to see my reaction. It absolutely hit that feeling of what it was back then.'

The music was created and supervised by David Holmes. The screenplay was licence to play in tunes from The Animals, Lee Perry and Suicide. And indeed, The Shangri-Las. The Good Vibes bands held their own while 'Laugh at Me' was kept back for the film's finale, the Ulster Hall scene from 1980. When Terri had recorded the song originally, they had added an orchestral version on the flip side, 'Laugh at Me (Again)'. It had sounded ridiculously lush for the punk era but in reality, Terri and his co-conspirator Geoff Harden had simply stolen the backing track from an instrumental album by Those Fabulous Strings, the MGM house band. David took this as a challenge and set up a live session in Los Angeles with quality session players, to make it freshly beautiful.

The film had an extraordinary sign-off as the credits rolled. Firstly, there were images of the original Belfast punks, pulling faces from another age. Quite a few of them had passed on, so this was in memoriam. The poignancy was underlined by the David Bowie track 'Star' from his Ziggy period in 1972. One of the characters in the lyric, Johnny, had joined the army and was patrolling the streets of Belfast.

The song had been suggested to David by Bobby Gillespie from Primal Scream. But it seemed like an unlikely choice, given the film's budget. 'The reality,' David explained, 'was we had no money.' They had already been priced out of using Them and 'Gloria' for the closing moments.

'We were just basically at the end,' he recalls. 'Doors were just closing. And Bobby just said, "'Star' by David Bowie". He said, "I actually know someone who knows him". And Gillespie recited the lyrics, and it had absolutely everything you'd want for the end titles. The lyrics were so resonant with what was happening in the film. It just summed everything up. Bowie was so admired by all the punks. It was one of those meant-to-happen tracks. We contacted David Bowie's management and he said yes, within three days. And he gave it to us for whatever we could afford. He was like, "I believe in the story, I don't need the money, this sounds like a great thing to be a part of. Of course you can have it."'

Carrie Davenport, courtesy Lyric Theatre

2018

ood Vibrations became punk rock theatre in September 2018, with significant noise and few resources. Cast members traded roles as Outcasts, cops, urchins and boneheads. Like the ingenious folds of a Good Vibes record sleeve, the Lyric Theatre stage became a rock and roll sinkhole, a Derry parlour, a backstreet and a killing field.

Glen Wallace and cast at the Grand Opera House, 2023.
Image by Carrie Davenport, courtesy Lyric Theatre.

The shuttered shopfront opened and a drum riser came hurtling out of the slot. 'Big Time' by RUDI announced the unbeatable subculture of Belfast in 1978. As with the film, the work was scripted by Glenn Patterson and Colin Carberry and the pace translated well. The direction by Des Kennedy was sympathetic to that. Terri received a fearsome kicking in the shop. The 1979 Good Vibes live tour was stopped by an incredulous squaddie who marvelled at this spike-headed crew and their cross-community import. As the musicians returned to the city, the skyline was flaming and injured and the audience was invited to grieve again.

Aaron McCusker inhabited the Hooley character. He was sensitive to the royal confusion of the man and did not seem overawed by Richard Dormer's intense manner in the film. Niamh Perry followed on from Jodie Whittaker's role as Ruth and a storyline that now acknowledged her own creative life as a poet.

The brute chauvinism of 70s Belfast was softened for the Lyric. The Gordy Owen role was assigned to an unnamed, female character. The history books did not quake at the revisionism but some punks were bothered by the ensemble version of 'Alternative Ulster'– transmuted into musical theatre and *Fame* dancing. The real Terri Hooley walked out after the curtain calls, to remind us that we were still subjugated by bigots, racists and homophobes. He inferred, rightly, that 'Alternative Ulster' was an unfinished business, rather than a song-and-dance routine. Albeit a highly popular one that rocked the box office.

There were plans to tour the production in 2020 but the pandemic delayed it for three years. Some of the cast returned for the Grand Opera House version in May 2023 and it was augmented by Glen Wallace as Terri and Jayne Wisener as Ruth. While the Lyric production wanted to avoid the 'musical' tag, it was now billed as 'The smash punk musical'.

Terri with Jimmy Fay and (above) with Lisa Barros D'Sa and Glenn Patterson.

There were added tunes from Protex ('I Can Only Dream') and Love ('Alone Again Or'). Fran O'Toole from the Miami Showband (murdered in 1975) was remembered with the swoon and mood changer of 'Can't You Understand'.

The show ended, as expected, with 'Teenage Kicks' and a knees-up. The production became tighter over the run and the final nights were keenly received. Yet it was also recognised that changes were due for the New York run at the Irish Center, part of a Tourism Ireland promotion in June and July. The ending became more nuanced and the production carried extra weight. The Americans (see the Greg Cowan testimony, page 126) liked what they saw. 'As much as 'Good Vibrations' is about Terri, its ultimate hero might be music itself, in whose saving, salving power he believes unwaveringly,' said the *New York Times*.

There was a perceptive note in the *Irish Central* review:

'Americans in particular will have a hard time understanding why Hooley repeatedly turns down easy money, success, fame, and all the usual rock and roll trappings in favor of one glorious night in the Ulster Hall when the bands he represents turn the Troubles and their attendant misery upside down.'

TERRI IS OUR LEADER

Terri on the opening night at the Lyric Theatre, Belfast, 5 September 2018. Image by Jim Core, courtesy Lyric Theatre.

Elvis From the Ashes

A problem with the Great Victoria Street site was the lack of a street-level window. They needed a signpost to direct customers up to the first floor. This was the topic for a late-night discussion in 1977.

'We were all smoking dope in our house,' Terri recalls. 'I said, "We need somebody that can point up to the shop – who's the most famous person in the world?" And somebody says, "Jesus Christ". I says, "We're not having *him* outside the shop". And then I went, "Everybody knows who Elvis is".'

So they commissioned two art school friends, John Waid and Leo McCann, to bring back the recently departed Presley. They chose a classic image, Elvis on *The Milton Berle Show* in June 1956, shaking his bits to 'Hound Dog' and confounding the nation.

Elvis was a much-loved piece of street furniture. The punks posed with him. The students, collecting for Rag Day, kidnapped him and demanded a ransom in return for his safe release. On one occasion, Elvis went missing and Terri found him hidden in the undergrowth behind the shop. Most likely, he had been stashed away, in preparation for a full disappearance.

ELVIS' ASHES

Elvis started rotting and eventually he was retired. Terri decided to cremate him and sell off the ashes as a sacred artefact. Unfortunately, there were few ashes left behind. So they sourced some ashes from elsewhere, mixed them, bagged them and 'Elvis' Ashes' became a popular sales item in the shop.

Elvis was recreated for the *Good Vibrations* film, a strangely emotional return. After shooting, he went on display at Terri's shop on North Street. When the shop closed in 2015, Elvis travelled to Lisburn, to live with Buck from The Defects. The rocker returned to Belfast a year later, badly decayed and requiring a radical knee replacement from handyman Billy Armstrong. Now, he is an essential part of the Belfast Music Exhibition at the Oh Yeah Music Centre in Belfast.

A third Elvis was created for the Lyric Theatre production of *Good Vibrations*. This was a rather stocky rendition of the legend but nevertheless he travelled to America for the New York production. When the lead actor Glen Wallace came back to Belfast, he brought a specially commissioned Elvis badge, which he presented to Terri during a visit to Bangor. A comeback special.

Hooley
Style

'**I** used to wear Doc Martens in the 70s. Especially to work, because I worked with chemicals when I worked for Kodak. I still have a pair somewhere. I got a pair of Doc Marten shoes given to me free when they opened up their new shop in Cornmarket in Belfast. I was asked to DJ at the opening and they gave me a pair of shoes. Later that night I went down Voodoo bar and Jonny Black, the bar man says, "You get new Doc Martens?"

They interviewed three people who were going to be doing design in the shop and said, "tell us about Belfast and what Belfast means to you?" And the first two people said, "Belfast shipyards" and stuff like that and the third one said that Belfast meant "Terri Hooley and Good Vibrations". And they said right, you're doing the job. And then they did a mural of me on the side of the wall in the inside of the Dr. Martens shop. My girlfriend went up and down the stairs a few times and never even noticed it until someone said, "what do you think of the mural of Terri?"

Hard men wore Doc Martens in the 70s and then punks started to wear them, but I started wearing them before the punks. It became a Northern Ireland punk look. On the first album cover of The Undertones they're all wearing them. The Clash wore them first, then The Undertones and The Undertones still wear them.

When I got the new DMs recently it took me a while to break them in. That was a memory that came back very quickly. They were hurting at the back of the ankles.

Since the 60s, I've worn jeans and crew neck jumpers 'cause I didn't like the idea of ironing shirts. Then I started wearing big overcoats when I was a teenager 'cause if I wasn't home by 12 o'clock I would get locked out so I used to sleep on people's sofas. Then I started living in an office on High Street on the weekends and started partying.

There was a whole lot of us in the 60s in McCann's clothes shop in Smithfield, they had these old bus conductor overcoats and we all went down and got them and they were really warm, especially in the winter. Because we didn't actually drink in pubs, we used to drink bottles of wine in Lavery's entry. And then my mate Tommy's aunty saw us one night with all these bottles of wine, so she sewed big patches inside the overcoats, where we could put our bottles of wine.'

'I would say I've never been as happy as I am now. Truly. I always had this empty feeling, a real sadness inside. For years and years and years. I think it stems back to my youth. People dying on me – it wasn't very nice of them to leave me on my own. And now it's gone. I'm very lucky that I'm so happy. And it's not a strange feeling. It only took me 70 years to be happy. I'm quite enjoying old age.'

Brian Young
Part 2

You can't keep a good man (or Terri Hooley!) down and during the late 80s and 90s he made several attempts to reactivate the label. Sadly, more often than not, these involved contemporary acts trying to cash in or gain media traction on the strength of the label's historical reputation. Terri took it all in his stride, remaining as enthusiastic and upbeat as ever – though I can't say that any of the acts he championed during those years did much for me. He never lost his knack for self-promotion and snappy taglines too – 'The North Will Rise Again' being just one example.

He continued promoting gigs too – the best for me being when he brought my longtime idol Mr Johnny Thunders to play Belfast in 1984. I'd seen Johnny play many times since 1978 and sorta knew him to chat to. I'd brought along a Marshall cabinet for him to use during the gig and musta got him to sign every record he ever made while we shot the breeze waiting for the soundcheck. The gig was one of those nights when everything just fell into place – the band were firing on all cylinders, getting called back for encore after encore. Afterwards, Terri took everyone out for a memorable slap-up meal in the fancy French restaurant in Shaftesbury Square. I spoke to Johnny about the Belfast gig in later years and he still remembered both 'that weird guy' Terri and the Belfast gig fondly.

RUDI split at the very end of 1982 – ironically, our most successful year by far – and after jumping ship from the ill-fated Station Superheaven, which got more record company money on the table in seven months than RUDI had in seven years, I'd thought I'd hung up my guitar for good – washed up, disillusioned and demoralised . Somewhat rudderless, a few years later, I put together a one-off bookzine *Automatic Shoes: A Tribute to Marc Bolan* and shifted all 500 copies almost overnight. It reminded me of the 'good old days', especially as it was printed by Dave at Just Books – and somewhere along the way I rediscovered why I'd gotten into music in the first place and I

started writing new songs before forming The Tigersharks, once described pretty accurately by *Hot Press* as 'Johnny Thunders fronting The Stray Cats'. The Tigersharks morphed into The Roughnecks before splitting and in 1994 I put together my current dream combo, Belfast's two-fisted greaser kings, The Sabrejets.

I'd never dreamt of playing old RUDI songs again but when Sean O'Neill and Guy Trelford published their exhaustively comprehensive book on Ulster punk, *It Makes You Want To Spit*, in 2004 and asked Greg Cowan, Petesy Burns and myself to play some old punk songs at the book launch at the Empire, it would have been churlish to refuse. The unfortunately named Shame Academy was the result and we headlined the event, knocking out spirited versions of several old Harp Bar faves with some RUDI/Outcasts numbers thrown in as well. There were other live sets that night too from fellow veterans of the punk wars including The Defects, Ruefrex and Mr Hooley himself. (Hilariously, Terri and I weren't speaking to each other that night as I had leased some live/demo RUDI material to a German label without his involvement.)

Johnny Thunders, Liz Young and Terri, 1984

The arson attack on North Street Arcade that gutted Cathedral Records was particularly devastating as Terri lost all his stock and had no insurance. It says a lot for the affection in which he is held that several old Good Vibes luminaries (Shame Academy, Undertones, Moondogs and Ruefrex) got together and staged a benefit 'Gig For Terri' at the Empire, which raised several thousand pounds, enabling him to open and stock a new shop in the Haymarket – fittingly christened Phoenix Records.

Since then, another benefit was held at the Mandela Hall, to celebrate the 30th anniversary of the release of 'Big Time'. This time round, Shame Academy, The Undertones and Panama Kings played to a packed house and compere on the night was celebrated local actor James Nesbitt, who read out a telegram from Bill Clinton congratulating Terri on his many achievements.

Terri and Shame Academy. Image by Stuart Bailie.

I have to admit that I was more than a little sceptical when it was announced that a film was being made based on Terri's life story – but my expectations were raised when I learnt it was to be directed by Glenn Leyburn and Lisa Barros D'Sa with music overseen by local legend David Holmes. I'd already worked with them on their previous film *Cherrybomb*, which featured The Sabrejets as the house band in a fictitious pub, The Lifeboat. That scene was filmed in the Rotterdam Bar, one of our regular local haunts, and I ended up playing guitar on and co-writing the music with David playing behind us on the film soundtrack.

I'd enjoyed that experience and when the *Good Vibrations* film was being put together, I was brought in to show the cast how to play the songs selected for the soundtrack not just by RUDI, but also The Outcasts and Undertones. Originally, it was suggested that the actors would sing and play the songs themselves – but thankfully this idea was scrapped and old live tapes of the original bands from back in the day were dusted off and used instead – though where no suitable tapes could be located I recorded new backing tracks with members of current combos like Colenso Parade and Cashier Number 9.

I gotta mention that Diarmuid Hayes who played me in the film insisted I showed him how to play the guitar parts of all the RUDI songs in the film and he learned them note perfect! I didn't see much of the actual filming apart from the final concert at the Ulster Hall, which brought back a lot of memories! Some pleasant – some not quite as much! I do have to say the chaotic 'Laugh At Me' finale with Terri onstage was handled really well and even this ol' cynic had to hold back a tear or two.

I got to see the finished film at the Ulster Hall premiere and to my undying relief it was MUCH better than I'd expected! As the onscreen caption as the film starts advises, 'based on the true stories of Terri Hooley', you know you're in for a treat! And while often factually inaccurate, it certainly does capture much of the underlying tension and sheer, breathless excitement of the time – and it has to be said that Richard Dormer's portrayal of Mrs Hooley's wayward

Brian and friends at the unveiling of the Harp
Bar plaque, 2012. Image by Carrie Davenport.

son is uncannily accurate, ably conveying Terri's charm, alongside his unquenchable optimism and lust for life. Truth be told, I thought he sounded more like the 'old' Terri than the current model does!

It was nice to see 'Wee' Gordy shown dragging Terri down to see us in the Pound (not the Harp!). I never expected people to take it as gospel but I shoulda known better – when The Undertones' Billy Doherty passed me on the way out of the premiere glowering and muttering under his breath, 'So you didn't like our trousers, then?' Er, I didn't write the script! But if the cap fits?

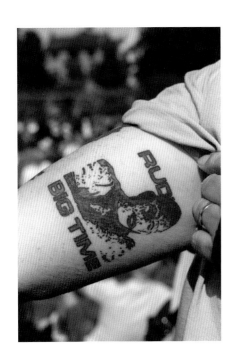

Bonus points too for featuring photographs of many of the real-life protagonists from back in the day alongside the end credits! I played the afterparty in the Black Box with The Sabrejets where everybody present said they loved the film – but I don't think anyone could have expected the glowing reception it received in the mainstream press and media nor just how successful it would turn out to be!

It is fair to say that the film gave Terri a whole new lease of life and a much-elevated media profile, which he thoroughly deserved. Sadly, this acclaim didn't translate into sales in the latest of his record shops in North Street. If everyone who gushed rapturously on social media about the great times they had in Terri's shop after the film came out had actually called into any of his more recent premises and bought something once in a while, then he would still be in business. So much for homegrown Norn Iron nostalgia!

I was even more surprised to learn that the film had been adapted for the stage and feared the worst. Thankfully, the cast had done their homework and in Aaron McCusker they had an actor again capable of capturing Terri's quirks and mannerisms while bringing his own considerable talent and personality to the role without lapsing into self-parody. It was refreshing to see more substance and depth given to Terri's wife Ruth and the hugely important and often overlooked part she played in the Good Vibrations story.

Despite some dubious wardrobe choices and a couple of cheesy quasi-'Kids from Fame' dance set pieces, the cast performed enthusiastically and musically hit the spot more often than not. I was grudgingly impressed – but I don't think anyone had anticipated the warmth and scale of the public reaction to the show as it played to packed houses, breaking box office records. Once again, Terri was granted another big bite of the media cherry – which he certainly made the most of – and why not?

The revamped stage show at the Grand Opera House just didn't work as well for me. Many of the key cast members had changed, not for the better, and the production appeared sluggish, lacking focus and sparkle – though I was relieved to hear that it had improved dramatically by the time it travelled to New York. Sadly, Terri's ongoing health issues prevented him accompanying the cast to the Big Apple which musta broken his heart.

I still bump into Terri regularly at gigs or out and about in his new, adopted hometown of Bangor. We've certainly had our ups and downs in all the many years I've known him but I'll always be grateful for the giant leap of faith he made, taking a bunch of semi-delinquent teenagers under his wing and enabling us not only to record and release our own records but also providing the initial springboard for both our local and national success, while making some (at least) of our dreams come true along the way. We spent a lot of time together back then and I learned an awful lot from Terri – both good and bad – even if I didn't always realise it at the time. Even when we were at loggerheads, I could never really stay angry at him for long.

Despite whatever differences we may have had, his heart was always in the right place and (for the most part) his intentions were good. I'm privileged and proud to be able to still call him a friend – just as long as I never have to listen to that damn poem ('Be My Friend') ever again!

Terri with Brian Young and Paul Rowan, Tower Records, Dublin, 1999. Image by Cliff Mason.

I guess the legacy of both Terri and the Good Vibrations label is that it proved that anyone can do anything if they put their mind to it – celebrating both the value of the DIY ethic and the power of self-reliance and initiative.

By putting out records by local bands on a local label that were every bit as good – and arguably much better – than those released elsewhere, Terri empowered people here, encouraging them to get off their backsides and do their own thing, not just in music but in many other fields as well. As a result, people here became more self-confident and self-aware, ultimately realising, if even briefly, that they were as good and as talented, if not more so, than anyone, anywhere else. Not something we were ever led to believe living here back then (or now…). As the chorus of the old RUDI song went, 'It's time to be proud'.

The bottom line remains that without Terri the Good Vibrations label would never have existed. RUDI, The Undertones, Outcasts, Ruefrex, Victim, Idiots, Moondogs, Protex, Xdreamysts et al. would have been consigned to the dustbin of history. Ulster punk would have been a lot poorer off and most certainly would never have had the impact it did either at home or further afield… and that's a simple fact! And the ripples are still being felt today! For all his faults (and they were and are many), we all owe Terri Hooley a helluvalot!!!

Brian Young,
14 September 2023

'I don't want to be like everybody else. I don't want to be a worker ant. I just want to have fun.'

Greg Cowan

What's the main theme about the Terri Hooley story? Okay, the punk scene was here, but without Terri, it wouldn't have been a punk scene. That's true. We were just various bands going about, no connection. He turned a lot of random bands into a Northern Ireland punk scene. He didn't do it for any financial gain in any way, whatsoever. And that's the main theme I take off it. Terri did this purely for his anarchist background, which he did enjoy. And helping out the kids.

He liked the mischief to a certain level. Some of us might have taken the mischief a little too far. At the end of the day, he did have a hippie background, with the love and peace there. The Outcasts pushed that slightly. Or friends of ours did.

But that is the basic theme. The film doesn't lie, as such. The play even less so. I think the play's better than the film. Not just 'cos there's more of my character in it. There seems to be an arrangement that whatever my character is doing, he just stays on stage!

I was shocked at how good it was in New York. I'd seen it at the Opera House and it was a wee bit disappointing. It seemed to be bloated. But they'd honed it down and they'd rehearsed for weeks. At the Lyric, they sounded like a band. At the Opera House, it sounded like a musical, but they got it back in New York. They listened to some of the complaints and I was genuinely knocked away by it.

Me and Yvonne went for the 'proper' premiere in New York. They had done about three or four performances before that in the Irish Center. The night before, I got up and sung with the crew at the Dead Rabbit bar. They were all harmonising to 'Self Conscious Over You'. They're unbelievably talented. They were sold out for five weeks, two shows a day...

In these circumstances, the legend becomes larger than the human being himself. But in this case, it surprised me how much of it is actually true, when you think about it. Did you ever imagine there would be a Terri Hooley industry? I mean, we really were looked down on, and there was no help from councils. There was no help from anyone. I think it's brilliant. Not just because of the added interest it brings to me and my career but he kind of did deserve it.

And it may be Hollywood-ised a bit, but it's true. I love the end of the play, especially in New York. It's just Terri in an empty room. It ends with 'Self Conscious Over You', believe it or not. 'Teenage Kicks' is used towards the end, but it actually ends on an ensemble version of 'Self Conscious Over You'. And then Terri's left on the stage and the lights go off.

I have more respect and I'm closer to Terri now than at any stage in my life. I like his company more. It's funny, there was a stage, maybe 20 years ago... when he was almost getting undue notice - 'Terri the Godfather of Punk', and stuff like that. Then it had gone the other way, and if not him – who? I think he's handled it very well.

And he's also not a bad DJ. I was really surprised at the last gig we did in the Limelight with him. It wasn't so much what he was playing – which also suited the crowd well. But as soon as the band walked offstage, Terri was ready and available, there were no gaps. I

Terri, Getty, Henry Cluney from SLF and Greg Cowan, Downtown Radio, 1983. Image by Alastair Graham.

Dylan Reid and Chris Mohan at the Grand Opera House, Belfast. Image by Carrie Davenport, courtesy Lyric Theatre.

went, 'You know, Terri, you've got really good at this'. He said, 'I'd like to think so – why is this a shock?'

Terri also didn't go looking for these things to happen. He didn't walk round saying, 'Would somebody please make a film about me?' But life is circular. You think about how unfashionable punk was in the late 80s and 90s. What did Terri do? He disappeared out of the scene. I think it's brilliant that he's now allowed to be a professional Terri Hooley. And I mean that in the nicest way. He doesn't have to be anything but himself. And he is feted. It isn't going away. I tell you what I really thought after New York: 'Where next?' I mean, I know there's the Irish connection, but when you see the guy out of *The Sopranos* who plays Christopher (Michael Imperioli) dancing to songs he's never heard before...

The *New York Times* review taught me something too. It was their play of the month. He said what he actually loved and what Good Vibes had captured – and Brian always maintained this – was that those first songs, 'Big Time' and 'Teenage Rebel', were a celebration of being young. When you saw them being played, it wasn't about Belfast. None of those songs were about Belfast. And he loved the fact that the play was about Belfast, but the music wasn't. It was just this celebration of being young and that energy. You watch an audience, who don't know any of the music... dancing! You're expecting it in Belfast. You didn't expect it in New York. There wasn't a punk in the room, apart from me.

So he isn't going away. After seeing it in New York, and seeing that version of it, where else could Terri's story go? It's a universal story.

I'm on a break from The Outcasts' world tour. Think about it: when we broke up (around 1985) we'd done gigs in France and a few gigs in England. This year, we're starting back in America and then Portugal, and Belgium to finish off the year. The plans are in for next year, and we're back to Japan. It's the most bizarre thing to ever happen to me. It's been brilliant for me, and not just on a personal level. I love being in a band. I also love the gigs we do. For the first time we've become a professional band. It's my job!

If the Good
Lord's Willing...

A t the end of every Hank Williams show, the singer would smile at his people, tip his hat and promise that he'd be back again real soon – 'if the good Lord's willing and the creek don't rise'. This was a familiar line in his home state of Alabama, meaning that the plans of mere humans were always contingent on bigger schemes. A natural disaster might cancel the entertainment and the workings of providence were always a mystery for the God-fearing sinner.

Hank had reason to be cautious because he was born with spina bifida and he managed the pain with drink and drugs. He was scheduled for a gig in Canton, Ohio on New Year's Day 1953, but the singer died on the road, in the back of his blue Cadillac, aged 29. He was dosed up on chloral hydrate, morphine and alcohol and his troubled heart had given in.

Terri had a gig poster of Hank's final booking on the wall of his record shop on Great Victoria Street. It was a reminder of the perils of the Lost Highway,

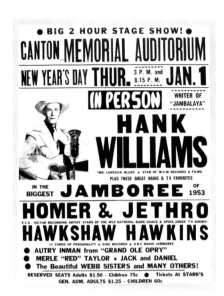

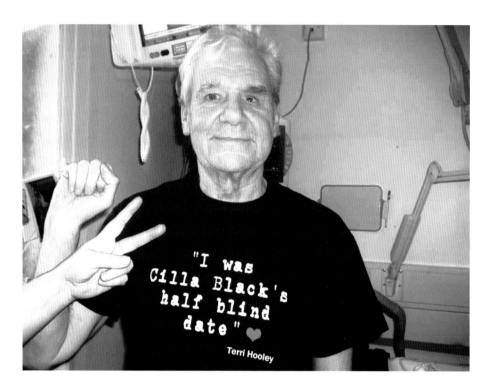

and it followed him around a few other shops. One of Terri's regular customers was an intense guy called Tom Jones. He knew everything about Hank and would argue the point with anyone who doubted him. Tom had visited the singer's grave at the Oakwood Cemetery in Montgomery. But the summer weather was punishing and Tom had collapsed from heat stroke in front of Hank's remains. He came home to relate the story but a few years later, Tom departed to Hillbilly Heaven and Good Vibrations was missing another character.

Terri reckons he lost 37 friends in 2007 alone. He was going to as many as three funerals a week. And then his parents died within three months of each other in 2009. Understandably, he was unwell, sleeping badly and drinking too much. He received some counselling and they said that he might need many more sessions, but he took comfort in a simple diagnosis. There was too much grief in his life and he hadn't had the time to process it. Once the extent of his loss had been unpacked and discussed, things were a little easier.

He had his reputation as a rocker and a bacchanalian. Yet when he was a young boy, he had wanted to be a missionary. In the 60s, Terri had gone searching for God.

'I used to fast and meditate. I found it very therapeutic. I did feel I was closer to God. Ray, the singing postman, used to do me meditation tapes. They worked. I went to a few meditation classes. I've always been searching for that spiritual side of my life since I wasn't going to church three times on a Sunday.'

To his great surprise, he found God, who appeared to him in a female form.

'So God told me to start eating meat again and start partying and drinking and terrorising the natives. I've done my best to do that. It was very loud and clear. I was living a pious life at the time. I had given all my property away, my posters and records.'

So that was his method afterwards. Still, he was surprised when his holy mission was interrupted by a heart attack in 1992.

'I'll never forget it. I'd been out late in the Rotterdam Bar the night before, drinking brandy. I was on the way down to work, I got the bus and went, I'm not well, I'm away home. I thought it was a hangover and then I had these pains in my arms and my chest. I phoned Eithne (Terri's then partner), who was the assistant chief social worker in the Royal (Victoria Hospital), and I says, "I'm having a heart attack, an ambulance is on its way". The ambulance didn't move outside our house for an hour or so. I got to the Royal and there was Eithne waiting for me. She says, "Are you all right?" I says, "I'm fine".'

Was Terri chastened by the experience?

'Aye, for about a week.'

On 26 August 2014, Terri came out of a DJ night at Lavery's and could barely breathe. His lungs were congested and his resources of strength were low. The doctor put him on a course of antibiotics and told him to stay off the drink. With great reluctance, he cancelled an appearance at the Electric Picnic festival that weekend. Four days later, he went ahead with a reggae set at the Limelight and introduced The Wailers.

He rallied a bit and, in September, he was off to Barcelona and a club date. He attended the San Francisco Film Festival and made his pilgrimage to the City Lights Bookshop. Then it was back to the late-night gigs: Tuesdays at Lavery's and Thursdays at Voodoo.

However, on Monday 1 December, he was admitted to the Ulster Hospital. For a week, his illness was a secret. He was planning to visit London for a punk gig at the 100 Club. The doctors said no, as the gravity of his illness became apparent. Heart surgery was very likely.

'I didn't believe them that I had a heart attack. I didn't have the pains in my arms and my chest. That, I knew all about. I said, "I want to be out of here by the 16th 'cos we've got the Good Vibrations Christmas party at the 100 Club", one of my favourite venues. They said, "You're going nowhere". So I cried for three days. And then I took really ill on the Thursday night. They said if I'd have been at home, by the time the ambulance came, I would have been dead.

'So I went, "Fuck it, I'm gonna be in hospital for a while, I'm gonna make the most of it" and I had a really good time. It wasn't boring and I had lots of visitors. I had good fun with my anarchist sign on the door and another one that said, 'Abandon hope, all ye who enter here'.'

His artist friend John Waid brought two T-shirts to his ward in the Ulster Hospital. One proclaimed that 'The Revolution Will Not Be Resuscitated' and the other said, 'I Was Cilla Black's Half Blind Date'. Terri's bedside became a lively social hub. Friends arrived with bottles of brandy and wine, even a bag of weed, which was discretely removed. He was photographed on the bed, getting fresh with Lady Portia. On the occasion of his birthday, a Skype link connected the patient to a crowd of well-wishers in his shop on North Street. They sang 'Teenage Kicks' for him and it felt like a rowdy remake of *It's a Wonderful Life*.

There was a fund-raiser at the Limelight in Belfast, 28 December. It was called 'Good Vibes for Terri' and the music community filled the venue complex, alternating on the two stages. Bronagh Gallagher and Tim Wheeler sang 'Be My Baby' and Duke Special played a resounding 'Old Man River'. The Outcasts and Brian Young's Sabrejets were representing the spirit of '78 and at the end, dozens of artists were on the main stage – including a few Snow Patrol faces and Bap Kennedy. They sang 'Teenage Kicks', with feeling. It had been rumoured that Terri was going to make a break from hospital for the finale, but sense prevailed.

Terri got his triple bypass surgery in February 2015. Shortly after he left the operating theatre, he insisted on having his photo taken. He was still wearing his green gown. He had an illuminated monitor device on his finger and he pointed it at the camera. "E.T. phone home," he said.

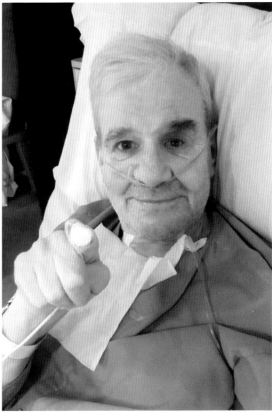

Claire Archibald

Stuart Bailie

His radio show goes online every Saturday night on Belfast 247 and gets a repeat on the Sunday. Terri puts the programme together at the kitchen table. Amber the rescue dog is normally at his feet – according to the presenter, she is there to fend off the supermodels who might be stalking him. Claire 'my glamourous assistant' takes care of timings and logistics, basically his producer.

He plays Judee Sill and Phil Ochs, The Maytals and Black Uhuru. Sometimes there's a random journey into Cajun country or a respite with Lee Mavers and the La's. He once themed an entire show based on the photograph he found of his 1966 record collection. Bob Dylan is a perennial, especially *Blonde on Blonde*, which he played obsessively in his 18th summer, a reverie of warehouse eyes and Arabian drums.

He gets messages from old friends in the Southern Hemisphere plus habitual listeners in Ballymena and Berlin. Michael, his sometime stage guitarist, sends

notes about the tunes that worked well and is critical of the poor selections. Terri tells rambling anecdotes and namedrops about encounters with Joe Ely and Bob Marley. There's a listener in Drogheda called Sherbie, who clears out the furniture in his kitchen and dances to the tunes. His dog used to join in the sport but sadly, Toby has gone and the music provides comfort.

Terri relates back to his pirate days with Harmony Radio, up on the Rocky Road in the Castlereagh Hills with his mate Tommy Lyttle. In the late 80s, there were cross-border runs to Dundalk for his reggae show on KISS 106. On many occasions he was pulled over by the army at the border. The soldiers wrote down their names and asked for requests. Sometimes the delay caused him to miss the start of the show. One night he arrived and the station manager was playing Eddie Grant and 'Living on the Front Line'. Terri read out the names of the soldiers when it was finished. They never stopped him again.

Recently, he heard 'Cottage in Negril' by Tyrone Taylor and he was taken by an acute memory. A middle-aged woman came into the shop with a bottle of wine. She said she wanted to thank Terri for the radio show. Her son and his mates would meet up on a Saturday night and listen to the KISS broadcast together in west Belfast. They might drink a few cans and have a bit of a smoke, but there was no harm in it. Another son had been involved in paramilitaries and was now imprisoned in the Kesh. The mother was glad that her younger boy had a different future, and music was giving him alternative ideas.

Behind his radio presenter chair there is an old poster of The Shangri-Las, a bill for a show at the Club Ponytail in Harbor Springs, Michigan. There's a hand-written dedication from Mary Weiss to Terri. She had heard about the *Good Vibrations* film and had contacted David Holmes, curious about the mention. He told her about Hooley's massive affection for the band and especially the song 'Past, Present & Future'. David invited Mary to the Belfast premiere of the film. Sadly, she could not attend but she sent her personal regards.

Terri gives shout-outs on the microphone to Brenda, Caroline and Laura. He remembers his own lonely times as a teenager in Hillfoot Road and the empathy has not left him. 'You may think that no-one loves you,' he says. 'But Terri Hooley loves you all.' He tells them to look after themselves, to look after each other and to look after the planet.

'And this crazy old fool with be back next week... if the good Lord's willing and the creek don't rise.'

Claire Archibald

Stuart Bailie

Stuart Bailie

Sixty years ago, he took his Dansette record player and a handful of 45s to the Strand Presbyterian Youth Club. Now he's on the payroll at Custom House Square in Belfast, 18 August 2023. His job is to warm up the thousands of people who have come to see Stiff Little Fingers and Peter Hook.

'It is fun,' he says. 'I'd be raging if I wasn't asked. And then I worry about it. I'm going, "Jesus, I'm 74 and I'm standing on this stage, what am I doing?" And then I go, "I'm getting paid for this. And I'm having a great time." It's great to see everybody and have a bit of a catch-up. I get all these people waving at me, people I haven't seen in years.'

He's got a set of Pioneer CDJs, a bottle of Jameson whiskey, a bag of tunes and a magnifying glass to read the small print on the record sleeves. He opens with 'Teenage Kicks' by Nouvelle Vague, a bossa nova version by some French people that Terri always enjoys. He plays The Damned, Buzzcocks and XTC, causing the punk pensioners to smile.

The former Sex Pistol Glen Matlock is also on the bill and he steps over to greet Terri. There were a few meetings in the past and talk of Hooley releasing one of Glen's songs as an Irish import on green vinyl. But then management got involved and the heart went out of it, so the deal didn't happen. That's irrelevant now and the two veterans share a respectful chat.

The arc of a Terri Hooley DJ set is about reaching The Undertones and 'Teenage Kicks' with as much delight as possible. Depending on the occasion, he'll play The Ronettes, The Foundations and The Clash. He is fond of Amy Winehouse and The Beastie Boys and he wants Pete Wylie's 'Story of The Blues Part Two (Talkin' Blues)' played at his funeral. There is always time for Pulp and 'Disco 2000', in which the boy wants his lover to return after a long absence. When Jarvis sings about the girl bringing along her baby, Terri cradles his arms and makes a rocking motion. We always laugh.

But 'Teenage Kicks' is the expected peak. He plays it late in the night when the joy is rising. The people applaud and they give him their energy. In turn, this revives Terri and he stretches his arms high, like an old-style union agitator. He has the style of Jim Larkin, leader of the 1907 Belfast Dock Strike, a tall man who took on the steamship companies and dissolved the sectarian divide that had weakened the workers. Larkin was also active at Custom House Square and his statue is below Terri's DJ podium, still raising the expectations.

We're also a few hundred yards from Corporation Street, where right-wing paramilitaries tried to abduct and murder Terri in 1976. Belfast has many conflict tales about horrific chance and lost lives. There are fewer stories about lucky escapes but when the two dockers rescued Hooley from the gunmen, part of our culture was better able to greet the rebellious future.

Arguably, it's a projection. Terence Wilfred Hooley was bullied at home and derided at school. He made a noise in the 60s, when the *Village Voice* misprinted his name and created an accidental brand. Terri mobilised the kids during the brief era of punk, but there was a long interval afterwards, when he spent decades in back bars, telling his stories and being tolerated, a Falstaff by the Blackstaff. Now he plays out like a national treasure, the stuff of mythology.

The actual person rolls with the fiction and is gracious with his laps of honour. He rejects the bigotry, bad faith, avarice and poor vision that damage our civic life. He is an unaffiliated, one-person revolution. His own way of life. Terri fucking Hooley.

Stevie Boy Nicholl

139

Good Vibrations: A Select Discography

SINGLES

GOT 1 RUDI – 'Big Time' / 'No. One'

GOT 2 Victim – 'Strange Thing by Night' / 'Mixed Up World'

GOT 3 The Outcasts – 'Justa Nother Teenage Rebel' / 'Love Is for Sops'

GOT 4 The Undertones – 'Teenage Kicks' / 'Smarter Than You' / 'True Confessions' / 'Emergency Cases'

GOT 5 Xdreamysts – 'Right Way Home' / 'Dance Away Love'

GOT 6 Protex – 'Don't Ring Me Up' / '(Just Want) Your Attention' / 'Listening In'

GOT 7 V/A – *Battle of the Bands* EP – RUDI, The Outcasts, The Idiots, Spider

GOT 8 Ruefrex – 'One by One' / 'Cross the Line' / 'Don't Panic'

GOT 9 The Tearjerkers – 'Love Affair' / 'Bus Stop'

GOT 10 The Moondogs – 'She's Nineteen' / 'Ya Don't Do Ya'

GOT 11 The Tee-Vees – 'Doctor Headlove' / 'War Machine'

GOT 12 RUDI – *I Spy* EP – 'I Spy' / 'Genuine Reply' / 'Sometimes' / 'Ripped in Two'

GOT 13 The Shapes – 'Airline Disaster' / 'Blast Off'

GOT 14 PBR Streetgang – 'The Big Day' (single-sided flexidisc)

GOT 15 Andy White – 'Six String Street' / 'Travelling Circus'

GOT 16 Cruella de Ville – 'Drunken Uncle John' / 'Those Two Dreadful Children'

GOT 17 The Outcasts – 'Self Conscious Over You' / 'Love You for Never'

GOT 18 The Bank Robbers – 'On My Mind' / 'All Night'

GOT 20 The Rainsaints – 'Caroline' / 'Would You Give Me a Chance'

ALBUMS

BIG 1 The Outcasts – *Self Conscious Over You*

BIG 3 The Nerves – *Notre Demo*

GOOD VIBRATIONS INTERNATIONAL

GVI GOT 1 The Bears – 'Insane' / 'Decsisions' [sic]

GVI GOT 2 The Jets – 'Original Terminal' / 'Block 4' / 'The Iceburn'

GVI GOT 3 Static Routines – 'Rock 'n' Roll Clones' / 'Sheet Music'

GVI GOT 5 Strange Movements – 'Dancing in the Ghetto' / 'Amuse Yourself'

GVI GOT 6 Zebra – 'Repression' / '931' (12-inch single)

TERRI HOOLEY: A SELECT DISCOGRAPHY

Terri Hooley – 'Laugh at Me' / 'Laugh at Me (Again) (Fresh, 1979)

The Legendary Rocking Humdingers – 'Dracula's Daughter' / 'The Hokey Pokey' (Bad Vibrations, 1982)

Terri Hooley – 'Big Time' / 'Red Cadillac and a Black Moustache' / 'Sins of the Family' (Immortal, 1999)

Various – *Time To Be Proud EP3* – includes 'The Cops Are Coming' by The Terri Hooley Experience (Time To Be Proud, 2012)

Terri Hooley – 'The Ballad of Good Vibes' (Parts 1–3) (Time to Be Proud, 2013)

Photo Credits

FURTHER READING

Bailie, Stuart, *Trouble Songs: Music and Conflict in Northern Ireland* (Bloomfield, 2018)

Bradley, Michael, *Teenage Kicks: My Life as an Undertone* (Omnibus, 2016)

Clayton-Lee, Tony, *101 Irish Records You Must Hear Before You Die* (Liberties Press, 2011)

Hooley, Terri and Sullivan, Richard, *Hooleygan* (Blackstaff, 2010)

Link, Roland, *Kicking Up a Racket: The Story of Stiff Little Fingers* (Appletree, 2009)

O'Neill, Sean and Trelford, Guy, *It Makes You Want to Spit: The Definitive Guide to Punk in Northern Ireland, 1977–1982* (Reekus, 2003)

A special thanks to Sean O'Neill and Spit Records (www.spitrecords.co.uk) for the tremendous punk archive.

Every effort has been made to trace the copyright holders of the images used in this book. I will be pleased to rectify any omissions in subsequent editions of this book should they be drawn to my attention.

Stuart Bailie
Front cover, 9, 11, 13, 15, 17, 19, 21, 23, 27, 29, 31, 59, 61, 98 (Good Vibrations shop, Bill Guiney), 99 (Alex, Phoenix Records, Howard St, North St), 100 (Eric Bell), 101 (arson protests, bottom row), 102 (Stuart's camera), 103 (Pete Doherty), 106 (shop), 107, 108, 112, 113 (Terri and Elvis), 115, 117, 119, 121, 123, 125, 127, 131 (Terri and Greg), 132, 136, 137, 138, 142, 143

Carrie Davenport
4, 30, 96, 109, 110, 122, 130

Claire Archibald
25, 114, 134, 135, 137 (Amber)

Alastair Graham
71, 77, 88, 129

Geoff Harden
72, 92, 93

Frankie Quinn
99 (Winetavern Street), 144

Cliff Mason
6, 124

Bill Kirk
36, 94

Patrick Simms
81, 82

Jim Corr
110, 130 (Lyric Theatre)

Larry Doherty
84

Steve Rapport
67

John Gilbert
52

John Carson
65
John T. Davis
91

Bradley Quinn
96

Stevie Boy Nicholl
139

Brian Young collection
74, 120

Good Vibrations film stills
105, 106, 113

Terri Hooley collection
33, 34, 35, 39, 40, 43, 45, 47, 48, 51, 53, 54, 55, 63, 68, 95, 98 (Good Vibes), 100 (Michael), 101 (top row), 103 (with Greg), back cover

Images by Stuart Bailie

There's no wave. There's new wave.

And there's Terri Hooley.

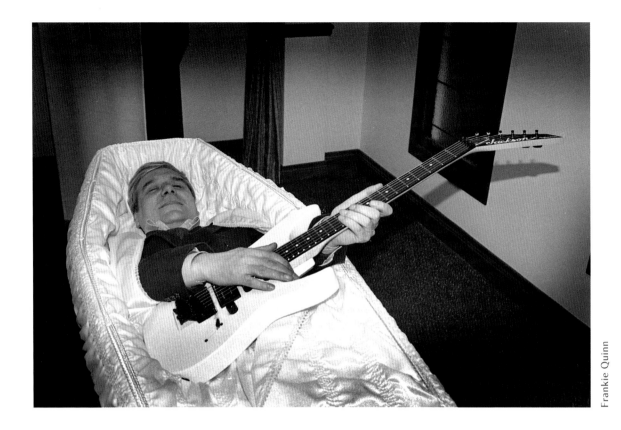

Frankie Quinn

Acknowledgements

I would like to thank Terri Hooley for being the best friend and for trusting me with his stories, company, tunes, philosophies and many laughs.

Once again, appreciation to Betsy Bailie for her great design work. Betsy also wrote the original piece on Hooley Style for *Dig With It* magazine.

Colin Harper has helped me through a series of books now, a massive asset to my DIY adventures in publishing. He's also a pain-free proofreader (belfastprooreading.com) and tolerates the sheer deadlines that I set myself and others. Likewise, Nick Garrad at Akcent Media is a patient and wise guide to the publishing process.

Claire Archibald has sourced images, prompted memories, eased schedules and has steered Terri away from the Lost Highway. We're all in her debt.

Thank you to the photographers: Alastair Graham, Patrick Simms, Carrie Davenport, Frankie Quinn, Cliff Mason, Bill Kirk, Steve Rapport, Larry Doherty, Bradley Quinn and Geoff Harden RIP.

Special Hooley insight from: Greg Cowan, Brian Young, Bronagh Gallagher, Ruth Carr, Dave Hyndman. Gratitude to Jimmy Fay and Glenn Leyburn. Good vibes to Maureen Lawrence, Damian O'Neill, Brian O'Neill, Laura Hale, Stevie Boy Nicholl, Sean O'Neill and Guy Trelford.

The Terri quotes have been sourced from dozens of personal interviews over several decades. My *Trouble Songs* book has been the foundation of a lot of the narrative. There have been various documentary projects along the way that have involved Terri. Regards to Ian Kirk-Smith, Mike Edgar and Vinny Cunningham for being on those rides.

Terri has often said that the Oh Yeah Music Centre (ohyeahbelfast.com) is a realisation of his youthful vision for the Belfast Arts Lab. I think he may be right. In return, Oh Yeah is a response to Terri's ideals for Good Vibrations and it was an honour to help create an exhibition cabinet and storyboards in the venue that celebrates the shop and the label. A salute to all the team on Gordon Street, especially Charlotte Dryden, Dee McAdams and Ryan O'Neill, who helped me to access the Oh Yeah archive.

To absent hooligans: Rosie McMichael, Gavin Martin, Dave McCullough and Carol Clerk.

Security by Amber the one-eyed rescue dog.

Catering by Skinner's of Holywood.

For Lily, Rosalie, Betsy and Collette.